WHAT MOMMY NEEDED TO KNOW

1/14/11

Jacqueline

Amazing. Yes God is so [...] in more ways than we can count. He has touched our lives. I'm so grateful. You were [...] for your support and knowing [...] 11 years old in Benton Heights. To think [...] High school - Wow! His providence [...] honored to know you. Enjoy [...] Blessings. Prosperity [...]

WHAT MOMMY NEEDED TO KNOW

What Future Mommies *Must* Know

Shirley Ann

To order additional copies of this book, contact:
Xlibris Corporation
1-888-795-4274
www.Xlibris.com
Orders@Xlibris.com
79981

CONTENTS

PART III

The purpose of this book is to assist others as they deal with life challenges on how to come out a victor and not the victim, especially mothers. It is designed to help future mommies pick up on the important things that my mother and I did not talk about. These things could make all the difference in the choices your children may chose or encounter in life.

It is my firm belief if mothers are honest with themselves, open with their children and willing to address the issues at hand without intimidation or fear, the family will function in a wholesome environment. This also includes the participation of everyone.

This book is not intended to discount the role or importance of fathers in children lives. Children are entitled to have both parents actively participate in their lives. However, the role of a mother is very significant because her relationship with her child begins at conception.

I will share with you how I answered when life called my name for particular situations and how my mother raised me. There will be times evident based on the choices that I made were due to the lack of my mother's training, teaching, love, and just having her presence in my life.

Often times I wanted to talk with my mother and share my true feelings but I did not know how to express myself. There were times that perhaps I felt I would be rejected or not believed. It was not the fact that my mother's actions made me feel this way, but mostly because of things happening in my life. There were certain little things happening in my head that impacted myself confidence, trust in others, and a need to belong. Now that my mother is no longer living I can only share it with her through this book.

Of course, I give my mother's sister, Aunt MaLou credit for providing a home for me and later my children also to live in that showed love and compassion based on her upbringing. Her upbringing in my opinion lacked open love for one another but again she did what she knew to do. My aunt not only lost her sister at an early age but she lost her father and mother days and months shortly after my mother died. It was hard times for our family. It appeared that my aunt handled all the family matters for everyone. This was a huge task. So, Aunt MaLou, I love you and say "thanks" for all you done for my children and me.

At the beginning of the book I will share twenty-eight important points on "what my Mommy needed to know" and "what I believe future mommies must to know." Towards the end of this book I will share portions of my autobiography intertwining the rest of my life.

This sharing will also offer further suggestions to mothers as they assist their children with decisions and choices in life. I am not blaming my mother for any of my choices; however, I am expressing the significance of having mother as a part of those choices.

Future mommies must know your children value your opinions, especially when solicited. The wisdom is for you to know when they are soliciting it whether through silence, verbally, or their actions. Mothers are chosen by God to fulfill the task of motherhood. Yes being a mother is a task that you cannot remove from your task list or just check the block. It requires daily activity and never goes away.

I became a teenage mother three years later after mom died. Based on my limited knowledge and the teachings mother left with me I did the best that I knew how raising my children. I am confessing that some of the things you will read in this book dedicated to my mom I repeated with my children. There were times when I should have listened, I should have been more understanding and certainly could have made better choices, which affected them.

What I have learned through life lessons is I did not have to do it alone. It's an awesome experience to be a mother and I didn't fail. I haven't mastered this task but I am still in the learn mode even with adult children. I am very grateful that I am a much better person, parent, mother, and now friend of my adult children. Now don't be misled I am still working on my relationship with my children and others. Yes, this task called relationship is on my daily list of things to do. These relationships will be addressed in the sequels to follow.

I also changed names of everyone mentioned except my mother and the man's name on my birth certificate to protect their privacy. It is my duty to honor each of them as I tell my story from my eyes. Let us take our journey into the life of Shirley Ann.

Foreword

To 100 Million Mommies,

Having coached superstar mommies like Lisa Nichols, Loral Langmeir, the Reverend Mary Morresy, and all best-selling moms as well, I've been waiting and waiting for Shirley Ann's book to arrive in final form. *What Mommy Needed To Know . . . What Future Mommies Must Know* precludes the epidemic breach of the priceless relationship between mother and child and family. The most important *ship* we all sail is inside our *relationship*, and no one told us how to be a great *crew* within that sail. Finally a book for moms and for dads on the cornerstone *relation ship* of *mom* is before the world, and in my opinion, publishing is issuing a true *historical event* with this book's release. In a career-driven hybrid family, full expression for woman global village, the topic of being a professional *mom* is being left by the old train station in a Star Trek Globalized World. Self Esteem Coaches like Jack Canfield, author of *Chicken Soup for the Soul,* and my Buddy Tony Robbins all are fanning the Mommy series because nothing is more important in the world today, nothing—not Dad, not the teacher, not the tutor, not the aunt, not the grandmother, truly not anything to equal our idea of *mom*. Dads need to magnify *mom* and cease depreciating *mom* in every respect if they want their child to have the most precious gift in the world, their future of *full potential.*

Our children are our future. This fact is not a maybe. Having worked a lifetime in public education to help with our schools (see *www.superteaching. org* or *www.ceopace.net* and our teen programs), we see the problems our children face, up close and personal. Over half our children in growing number of school systems nationwide (the largest of these) no longer complete even high school. *Mom* is the key, not education.

There is an epidemic of abuse, verbal and physical, taking place with our children, which I see in our Teen Feast Class. Twenty years ago when I launched Feast, I had no idea these problems even existed having had a (sorry, I'm dated) "leave it to Beaver" family upbringing in San Francisco in the 1950s. In an entrepreneurial age where 55 percent of all employment opportunity is *self*-employment versus employee-based employment, the family is the only instruction that matters for this career path option—the best option within the Age of the Entrepreneur. As school, in conventional terms, does not prepare the learner to advance into the entrepreneurial full-partnership economic opportunities, where is the education that values *dreams* second only to relationship? Who can teach that baby girl or that young male growing up how important *their dreams* are if not *mom* as the core teacher in the home? Mom has to inspire the culture of *dreams* as their first job and find their own way to *joy* and *balance* as their second. Without a GPS for *moms*, which you're about to download all the current maps for, how would a *mom* navigate to her destination in today's world?

Until Mommy was published, there was no *tool kit* for the modern mom. She is left reading old maps in a GPS-under-construction, detour-filled *mommy* freeway system. Dr. Schultz and all the rest are important, if not somewhat dated in today's family communities. Mom faces a faster pace, more choices, more financial constriction (as our middle class in many competitive capital economies is disappearing) into pressure. Moms under pressure have tough missions to *not show* their pressure to their young adults just entering discovery and dream building. Showing that their dreams are their life as "the full house" for the next generation is mom's mandate. But *how*? Where is that missing GPS for *mom*?

That is where Mommy Shirley comes into our lives and why, as a multiple best-selling author and superstar of *Tapping the Source*, I step out to encourage as a father of *nine* with two adopted children that every single *mom* on the planet read *What Mommy Needed To Know . . . What Future Mommies Must Know*. I've been divorced. More than once. Dads, we all need this book too. It is so important to *our* babies we father along the way. We don't need to fix mom, we, as "fixers" by nature, need to find new ways to encourage and support *mom* fixing herself. That is what relation-ship in great parenting is all about. We are all crew, and we cannot get off our children's ship in their entire lifetime. We will always *be* Mom and Dad. You must, in my opinion—as a world family change agent—advocate and move to pass this book on as their gift to ten moms you know. I encourage readers to host Mommy Parties and give the book away at each Mommy Party as you pay it forward (really) and pass great *mommydom* forward so that the all-time best-selling Mommy book on earth is grassroot shared and cared for.

The sand leaking through our hourglass egg timers this minute is the sand of our children's *lives*. We simply cannot afford to not compress this sand to D flawless diamonds in a way we all only wish we could have enjoyed when we all grew into our own dream work of full potential. If we could only all do it over. If you begin doing anything thing this book suggests, embrace the confirmation and transfer it by paying it forward as you host your own Mommy parties. If your life begins to be transformed into new a mommy life of renewal of balance and of *joy* by reading this book and your children are the masterpieces in part because you took time to underline make notes and, most important, *take action* in your life, you go the extra mile to share with other moms as you become the example and host your own world Mommy Parties. That is my request related to how important this reading has become to so many mommies.

But remember, as you read, when it comes to your children and their lives, their innocence, their full childhood, and the *dreams* of our unborn generation, that next child impacted by Shirley Ann's book simply *cannot* wait or have their full potential be put off until *we* are ready. There is urgency in your *joy*—both yours and theirs—real urgency in the world.

I bring you my strongest endorsement, and I have endorsed some huge best sellers like Lisa Nichols's *No Matter What* (one-million-dollar book advance, see Lisa thanking me on video online at *www.ceospace.net* by scrolling down to the video entitled "CEO Space: No Matter What with Lisa Nichols. SUPERSTAR Endorsement Video—ideal for authors and artists", William Goldstone's smash back-to-back *The Twelve,* and bigger than *The Secret,* "*Tapping the Source,*" released in late 2010 to reshape the world. Both Bill and I agree with *Tapping the Source,* that *mom* is the one essential transformation the world needs to step into cooperative capitalism, the better future we all desire, and a way of life that only *mom* can bring to the world, which remains a timeless principle.

The ancient writing all suggests the first commandment, Mommy, is to love yourself even as you love the Lord thy God . . . and close behind is for the child command to *honor* thy mother.

You're about to read the source book of the *law.*

With great affection and respect for mommies of the world,

Berny Dohrmann
Chairman of *www.ceospace.net*

PS: You are reading the most important book for the children of world published in this decade—following my endorsement for *Chicken Soup on Parenting*—and *When Mars & Venus Collide* by John Grey. I'm sure the readership of this book (including dads) will pass them all with your recognition how important Mommy is to share and pass along in a world buzz that has no end . . . thinking always of that one next CHILD.

The Lessons Begin (Prelude)

Have you ever done something, and then you were ashamed of the decision you made? Why were you ashamed? Mother you need to know that I wanted to fit in, so I must confess I have done things that I was ashamed of. As I forgive myself, as your daughter I am also asking you to forgive me.

Mothers, "forgiveness" is an opportunity to have a new beginning or a "fresh" start in life. Be sure to practice forgiveness with yourself so you are able to forgive others, foremost your children. Forgiveness gives us a direct passage to true unconditional love.

Did you ever measure your actions against someone else's standards? Were their values different from your value system? Of course that difference could not be the reason why you felt what you felt. Mommies must teach their children how to be confident, courageous and bold within themselves. This doesn't mean they are cocky, arrogant or disrespectful. Moms it is important for you to show your little prince or princess their true value. Mothers must teach their children regardless to what others may say or think about them, they have the final words and ultimate decision.

Does embarrassment haunt you, your mind, heart, your very being? Things like when your stomach begins churning as if you were about to become sick when they show up or are exposed. Was it because you were attempting to please someone else and later found out that it didn't really matter at all?

There was no way you missed the mark of making that person happy. Yes, it is possible that you missed the mark. The world does not have to stop because you missed. Actually, it doesn't stop. All you have to do is not stop, start again, and aim higher looking dead at the bulls-eye. Yes, become laser beam focused on the task of motherhood. It is an awesome task and you are the perfect fit. I am encouraging you to be all you can be and be your best.

Our children seek and need our approval. We can either build them up or tear them down. So are you feeling as though the choice you made at the time was a good one, only to later learn that others would ridicule your choice? Well, don't feel alone because I too have been there and done that! What future mommies must know is teaching your children how to value their uniqueness is a major key to them having great self-esteem.

Being ashamed is rarely received in a positive manner. The term itself, broken down, often refers to a sense of remorse or feeling of guilt about an action taken. The interesting thing is everyone at one time has experienced this feeling in his or her lifetime. Of course, there may be an exception to this statement; however, I say keep living and your experience will definitely happen. There is one thing that I offer for you to keep in mind: what really matters is *how you respond*.

Mom you taught me how to hold within myself what I was feeling. I now know this is not always the best way to handle things. I need to know what to keep inside of me and what to tell others. Nonetheless, it's okay though because I accept you only taught me what your mother taught you. Another thing you taught me was I am in control of my actions and feelings. No one else is to blame if I act out of character.

Do you sometimes stay stuck in the state of mind that it is someone else fault why you did or did not do something; or do you acknowledge it, accept it, make the necessary adjustments and move on without blaming someone else? Let me assure you that you are not the first individual to have had that experience. Unfortunately, you will not be the last. My encouragement to you is to acknowledge it, accept it, make the necessary adjustments and move on towards your purpose. Every step we take in life is a lesson learned leading us to our life purpose.

Just breathe, ah . . . it really is life just happening and unfolding. Do you realize that the rule of thumb is more than likely someone else has already had that life experience? You have been chosen for such a time as this. It does not matter what you're experiencing just know that there are a set of "footprints in the sand" carrying you on and through your journey that are not yours.

We can choose to learn from someone else's experience, which can be a valuable experience because it can save us unnecessary pain and definitely time. Experiences impact and shape our very being to the core.

Mom I believe you wanted to spare your three daughters: Natashae, Shirley Ann, and Irene the pain you went through. It is so unfortunate; however, that we have experienced a lot of pain since you left our lives at an early age. What I am sure you are aware of as you look down from heaven on us is you taught us how to survive by looking into our eyes when we were children telling us we can make it. Guess what, Mom? We are survivors.

It has been said to write things out and make it plain for others to read, heed, and learn prior to them having that same experience. Or the other unfruitful option is to experience the pain and wonder why it hurts because we chose not to listen.

Let me encourage you to put the book down, get a sheet of paper or even your journal, find a pen or pencil, and begin to transform what is in your mind to paper. I have also included space at the end of each chapter for you to jot down your thoughts as you reflect.

Go ahead and get uncomfortable or comfortable depending on how this affects you. Write down some of the things you need to talk about with your mother or children that you have not shared knowing that all is well. Write down things you know they should know that could make their lives possibly a little bit easier. Share with them your pain but always show them your strength and how they can overcome any situation because Mommy is there to listen and support.

Listening is a skill, its an art. It is not prejudging or deciding how the person should solve their challenge. It is not thinking up what you want to say while they are sharing. True listening is being open, giving your full attention and seeing it not only from their eyes, but also seeing it sincerely from their heart.

We all need someone to genuinely listen to our heartbeat. What's your pulse rate? Are you safe? Is it beating normal, how about your children? A healthy pulse rate is good for the heart. Ask your doctor, better yet ask your mother if they agree with this saying. Actually, mothers really do know what's best. The Creator has equipped mothers with a special sensory perception.

I know what I have asked you to do can be a challenging task for some. You are not alone. I too have been there and got that tattoo. You know the tattoo of being afraid to share things with my children about my life, my true feelings about their decisions, and our family in the spirit of love and not control. Oftentimes I was afraid because I didn't know how to say what I was truly feeling. I had incompleteness happening in my life. I am not proud of that decision but what I do know is I am not alone. Mothers have a lot of things in common. We are real people, with real problems, seeking reliable solutions.

Mothers are leaders, guiders, nurturers, the pillow where children want to lay their head and worries knowing that no one else would understand them like Mother. I realize many of you are carrying out your roles with little or no problem. However, do you have your partner, the man who fathered your children assisting you as you raise your children? How many mothers know how to tie your son's tie for the school play? Believe me when daddy does not step up to the plate and assist by carrying out his role, the family can and does comes up short.

Mothers it really is about sacrificing and giving yourselves for the love of your children. I commend those of you who have done this without condition. I understand there is always an agenda. The question at hand is whether or not your motives are for the betterment of the children or you. Well, as I think about it, you really don't have to choose either or because you can have both. Most importantly I want to point out is if you find yourself in a position where you do have to chose, then chose for the betterment of your young children. They depend on you to make quality decisions on their behalf. We have to save our children from self-destruction.

What I realized was until I made up my mind to do different, I stayed stuck. I stayed in a condition that wasn't beneficial for all. What I have learned is being stuck really does hinder our movement and our visualizations from becoming our reality.

So, yes go ahead jot down those ideas now, or while reading the book, constantly pray about them, get in the right frame of mind, and condition allowing your heart to pour out with the intents of building a loving family. Give your mind and heart a cleansing. Voila!

Yes, you are looking at your ideas and thoughts expressed on paper! You did it; you took a step to manifesting your dreams, creating them to become a reality. You can absolutely have a healthy and wholesome conversation with your children. Congratulations on taking this necessary step by opening yourself up to living your dreams with your children. Never let anyone tell you there's no hope for your children. You are their hope.

As a reminder, ensure ground rules are set on how you and your children can have a quality conversation with respect for all parties up front. Also allow your children the opportunity to share their dreams, their desires, their wants, their expectations, their disappointments, and their dissatisfactions without judgment and criticism. Listen for the heartbeat of their hearts as you share your lives together on the same team. Our children need you in their lives, Mom. Mommy! Where are you? I need you in my life to show me how . . .

Thank you for taking this journey with me as we walk the trail of *What Mommy Needed to Know . . . What Future Mommies Must Know*. I hope what I share invokes you to take an internal look and not solely external. It is my intent to share how you can develop a holistic and healthy relationship with your children based on my personal experiences.

I looked internal, and this book was birth as a result. I don't blame anyone for any of the choices I did or did not make. What I did recognize is having my mother in my life was very important and necessary.

Mothers are placed on this earth to assist their children through the process we call life. Fathers are placed here to assist and be the substance that is in the glue which causes it to stick or bond things together. Children are the puzzle pieces used to complete our family process and then the cycle repeats itself. Is your puzzle complete, is it sticking together and placed in a frame creating a picture that you want to hang in your home so others can admire?

It is important for the cycle to not just repeat itself through trial and error. No, this cycle must entail lots of love, wisdom, understanding and purpose benefiting humanity at large. Mothers and fathers, are you truly answering your call of destiny so you can empower your children to answer as destiny calls them? Puzzles are not complete unless all the pieces are present and properly connected sealed with glue.

What Mommy Needed To Know . . .

What Mommy Needed To Know . . .

What Mommy Needed To Know . . .

Part I

What Mommy Needed To Know . . .

The Beginnings of an Unknown Journey

I was born on June 10, 1958, in a little town called Benton Harbor located in the great state of Michigan. On my birth certificate, it says I was born to Dave Martin and Oletha Glespie. One very important thing happened the day I was born. What was that you might ask? Well, I got to meet mother. Yes, having my mother in my life meant the entire world to me. Mothers are important and significant in children's life.

Unfortunately, I do not recall having my father or the man's name on my birth certificate in my life as a role model. I presumed Dave was already deceased, so I did not get to meet him; neither did mother talk about him to me, and for some reason, I dared not ask. It would have been great to have my father in my life, but having Mother present and accounted for was essential and not an option.

Point #1 What mommy needed to know: *Mom, you need to know that I am grateful that you decided to give birth to my life by keeping and not aborting me. Thank you for life and having that life with you as my mother. It was important you were there for me, but it would have been great for my father to be there for you and me.*

Point #1 What future mommies *must* know: *First, your children can only live physically if you decide to birth them into this world. The decision is probably ultimately yours; however, you do have the power to choose life for someone else. Next and most important is you also have to power to show them how to live life to its fullest. You have been chosen to connect at the navel cord with those children.*

What Mommy Needed To Know . . .

What Mommy Needed To Know . . .

What Mommy Needed To Know . . .

Is It the Truth or A Lie

Later on in my life after Mom died, others told me that a man named Nathan Johnston was my father and not Dave Martin. Being told this by others and not my mother really confused me. It was hurtful and I really felt alone. Here I am, an eleven-year-old girl with a lot of problems already before I became an adult. Why? I wondered back then why this became my fate, but now I know. This became my fate so I could share and help someone else make it through life challenges regardless of the situation.

Nathan did not play a very active role in my life even though I got to meet him. I do recall going over to his house spending some time with him and his wife. It was as if he was content with me coming by every now and again. He wasn't footing the bill of being a parent.

I wanted a father in my life, so I guess as a child, I was just as content. Nonetheless, there was still this uncertainty about him being my father, but I never questioned it. After all, I can recall back during those times, Black children rarely questioned their parents. Let me clarify that this could have been the case in any other family, but I am speaking about my experience.

Lord, what's going on today? I won't judge whether that was good or bad, but I will say "respect" is just that—R.E.S.P.E.C.T. Too many of our children have lost respect for their elderly, including moms. There is little or no respect among people as a whole because people disrespect one another all the time. We live in a selfish society. As a result of the various challenges in life, many mothers feel they need help raising their children in today's society.

I agree with mothers that they need help raising their children; however, it is the mother and father's primary responsibility to raise their children. Parents are told to train up their children in a manner of self-respect, dignity, trust and the like. Instead of this happening with genuine love, many children are known as latch key or techno children. There is no one home to teach them how, so it is left up to computers, games, NBC, CBS, ABC, MTV, and different record labels, just to mention a few things, to raise the children. The problem with this system or this tool is their values just might not be the values you want your children to learn. Who is censoring what they are teaching your children?

Many mothers are required to work outside of their homes to provide for their children basic necessities. We are loosing our family values fast due to mother's lack of presence in the home teaching and training her children. Often times this is because she has to go to work outside of the home to provide for her family. Many mothers are now seeing the detriment of this decision, so they are becoming entrepreneurs bringing themselves back into their homes to raise their children.

On the other hand some have joined the military hoping to provide security for their families during this recession. Ultimately, in today's military she looses sight of being in the home raising her children because of her being sent off to war. Yes, the children loose out on mommy's presence. I salute our single parents and dual military family members for their service. While serving myself as a leader I often wondered how you were able to provide a quality life without your presence for your children as myself. I too spent a lot of time out of my home providing for my children using this same resource. I must say that this resource certainly provided for my family both financially and as well as in other positive ways but, my children were not necessarily first place in my life because I had a "mission" to fulfill. *Of course, you know this is another book in the making.*

Yet it is unfortunate that there are also those moms who are just giving up and quitting on her children. This recession has impacted the family drastically. We need our father's in our family so mom's can do her due justice in the homes. Today's families are built different than they were in the past. The demands and focus in raising our children are certainly different because the basics just aren't the basics anymore. Moms we must stick through the tough times and know there is hope. We must bond together and share with each other the secrets of keeping a family together. The time is now more than ever that our older women must come forth and teach the younger women how to properly raise their children as they were taught. Now I realize some things have changed with times, but instilling good quality values in our children are essential and necessary.

There is no one accountable of the family because most anything goes when mom is not there to monitor her home. As the old saying goes, "when the cats away the mice will play". Children have to constantly fend for themselves. No country will survive or stand who leaves it up to future generations for solutions without proper guidance and direction being taught to them in our homes. We are calling on all dads to assist mom in raising our children.

The truth is our children are facing many challenges unlike their parents faced. Decisions that children are making today are being paid at adult prices. This price is too high for anyone to pay especially our most precious resource. There is no price good enough to exchange for our children. The Dow Jones is up and down, perhaps this is okay for some. It is not okay for our family matters to be worse off than the stock market or big business. It is time for the people to stand together and stop the violence in our homes.

The truth matters if your family is not facing crisis because perhaps you are instilling the right values in your children. However, the greater truth of this is it really matters more if other families are facing crisis to your family. It matters because your children can become a statistic or a victim of abuse based on wrong relationships formed. It matters most because we are one big family living in different houses. We all want and are entitled to having successful homes.

Unfortunately children are bullying one another because of material things, different values, they are being taught racism and prejudice in their homes. They are being taught to bring harm on one of their peers is the right choice. This is brutally wrong. There must be change in the mindset of our parents, more importantly our children. Who is teaching your children what is right or wrong? What is truth or lie?

The truth is there is a war right here also on US soil that the terrorist are winning. This war is waging against the children, against mothers, and against fathers commonly called "the family". Mommy and daddy put on your war clothes to fight the enemies of suicide, gang killings, bullying, disrespect, homelessness, despair and hopelessness in the family. Your war clothes consist of love, patience, gentleness, meekness, kindness, peace, understanding, wisdom, tolerance, communication, and strength to mention a few important missing clothes in the wardrobe.

The lie is your children don't love you or want to listen anymore. The lie is your children have A.D.D. or some other disease, so give them a pill. The lie is someone else can do a better job than you. There are so many lies being told but the most fatal lie is it takes a permanent decision to remove a temporary situation because no one cares.

Well I say the real truth nothing but the whole truth is we all face challenges. Let's rally together and beat this unseen terrorist that is wiping our families off the earth. The greatest weapon we have is unconditional love. Let's use this weapon of love as the ultimate weapon of mass destruction against hatred worldwide.

What Mommy Needed To Know . . .

What Mommy Needed To Know . . .

What Mommy Needed To Know . . .

Uncertainty Does Not Solve the Unknown

Have you ever wondered about something but you were too afraid to just ask somebody? Certainly, you have crossed that bridge. Or are you still on the bridge afraid to cross? We all at one point or another probably have had the experience of this uncomfortable feeling. *Wow!* Is all I can say right now, but it is what it is.

Unfortunately, today I still feel somewhat incomplete because I really don't know who my biological father is based on DNA testing or even him assuring me through his actions. As I mentioned earlier I don't recall mother having that important conversation with me either.

I cannot even relate to my father's side of the family because I do not know who you are. Girls need their daddy's too. One of daddy's role should be the disciplinarian. Another is him showing her how a real, genuine, and mature man should treat her.

Discipline should be given appropriately with love and affection. We discipline our children because we love them. Dads are positioned as her first love, the first man in her life. He should be there to reinforce mother with the children whether or not the adults continue in their relationship. Unnecessarily some children are deprived of both parents because adults can't properly sort their difference for the benefit of the children. Do your children have access, the passport to both mommy and daddy's love unconditionally and know it?

Point #2 What mommy needed to know: *is my father missed a great opportunity to be a part of my life because of a decision you and him made without my consent if he was alive at my birth. I realize I was just a child but I too was wired to understand something such as I have a mother and a father who loved me at all cost. He should have been there to support me with or through you.*

Point #2 What future mommies *must* know: *is you should have a working relationship with the children's father for the sake of the children. They should know their father. Your children are individuals with thoughts, ideas, and aspirations. Understanding the chemistry and makeup of children can channel them in accomplishing positive things. You teach your children how to agree to disagree in a healthy manner.*

I cannot say it enough about how important it is for boys to have their fathers in their lives. Mothers are wonderful and we can raise our boys to be gentlemen; however, contrary to popular belief we really cannot raise them to become men without men. I know many women might disagree with me but the truth be told we have different skill sets as men and women. Our chemistry is different. Children were not intended to be raised in single parent homes. Challenge the fathers to come and treat you like queens by assisting you in their proper roles as kings. By the way, only another man who is a truly king has the formula to show another man how to be a king; thereby, knowing how to treat you the woman, mom as a queen. Again that's whole different book in the making.

Someone reading this might ask, "What's the big deal, Shirley Ann?" My question to you is, "Do you know who your daddy is, and is he involved in your life?" How about your children? Do they know who is their father because you told them?

Mother's can raise their children; however, they cannot effectively raise them alone. There must be a support system. It does take a village to raise children but their parent, both father and mother should be the first in line if they are still living. Assume your responsibility. Accept the choice and consequence of your decision by raising your children. It is your duty and an honor.

How do you truthfully feel about your answers? Will you come out of hiding and tell me? Hush . . . keep your mouth closed, Shirley Ann, I can hear you saying, "No can ever know how I truly feel. Will they understand or just judge me?" If you tell your true feelings, will you become the "outcast?"

My suggestion to you is to not worry about it, go ahead and free yourself today. Do not let anger or embarrassments blind you. Sometimes you only have to jump start the battery in a car to get the vehicle started in order to get to your destination of choice. Start your healing process so you can jump start, your future NOW. You can make a difference in your life. You can also make a difference in the lives of others . . . most importantly your children. Your gifts are counting on you to release them in this earth realm. It's never too late to take action. What is your destination?

I heard the renowned Mr. Les Brown describe a scene where an individual was lying on their death-bed with all their gifts and dreams standing around discussing why they were never put into action during the times when the individual was healthy. The gifts and dreams were crying, complaining, aching, and dismayed because they were headed to the grave with the responsible individual without choice. They were never used. Don't die with your gifts and dreams within in. Let them live. They cannot be manifested through your children because they have their own.

Your children need you as an example to show them how to put them into action. People are waiting on you; yes your children are counting on you to make positive decisions displaying how they can do the same when life shows up by positively answering the call of destiny.

Does it really matter what someone else has to say? My vote is, "Yes, it does matter"; however, in a more vote of confidence your opinion counts more than anyone else when it is all said and done. You are the most powerful person in your life.

Of course it is wise to seek out wise counsel; but the choice is up to you so choose wisely. You cannot be both right and wrong at the same time. Mothers we must share this important point with our children in love. You have the power to raise your children as my mother raised me to the best of her ability.

It is true that the pain I have endured regarding this situation of not being told about my father from mom is unspeakable, very unexplainable. I have bored this pain my entire life. I am asking you current mommies to take action now if you have not by talking with your children about tough matters!

Moms there are many children who are finding themselves in unspeakable and unexplainable situations. Help your child by reaching out through understanding. My therapy has been that I was able to accept it and just numb the pain as I moved on with my life. It wasn't the best decision some might say but it was my best alternative during those times so I thought.

Certainly, I had to choose to not stay stuck, crawl up and die. I chose to jump start my life. Yes even though I have the memories and scars, I am beginning to love life every day. I have learned how to value the scars by not despising humble beginnings.

This is a painful process but I accept I must get through it. Exactly, mothers we must get through our deepest hurts and woes. Our children are depending on us to perform our duties to the fullest, with pride and our best foot forward. Choose to live . . . live for . . .

Oops, I forgot to remind you to not forget it is not just about you or me, but it is about teaching and living for the generations to come after you and me. What do we tell them? No not only what do we tell them, but how do we show them?

Do you remember "Show and Tell" during your early school years? We are their greatest example. The question is, "Are you going to tell the truth, nothing but the whole truth, so help you God?"

Are you standing in the front of the line, in the middle, in the back or you are in total denial and decided to get out of the line? I beg you to take your rightful place. I beg because your children are important. I am speaking this request from the voice of a child. Get in and stay in line.

My mother is now deceased and she cannot physically change any feelings that I have or bring any closure for me during a sit down session between the two of us. However, unlike my mommy, you can make a huge difference and take your place at the table of discussion. Get in the front of the line to fight for your children. Act! Act despite of fear, doubt, worry, tiredness, or whatever might be holding you back. You are empowered to raise your children. Tell them what they need and must know to contribute positively to society.

I am now faced with the question, "How can I explain this uncertain thing that has happened in my life without my choice to generations after me?" I was just a kid, you know. The moral of this is I am really not sure if I ever met my real father or not.

Point #3 What mommy needed to know: *Mom, you need to know that I hurt on the inside because I cannot connect my roots. It hurts because I do not ever recall hearing the truth from you.*

Point #3 What future mommies *must* know: *Your children are entitled to know who their biological father is from you. Your truth can save them a lot of unnecessary pain. Let them hear your voice and not the voice of an outsider, someone who wasn't even present during conception.*

What Mommy Needed To Know . . .

What Mommy Needed To Know . . .

What Mommy Needed To Know . . .

The Pain of Not Knowing the Truth

As I look back over my life I ask myself why I didn't pursue the truth about my natural birth father. Why didn't it matter to me who was my real father, or did it? Should daddy have stepped up to the plate and ensured I knew who he was? Is it the family's responsibility to say what mom or dad did or did not say? Perhaps, my parents just could not say it or never thought I would want to know. I am not certain why they would think I would not ask or want to know, but guess what? They were partially right. I did not ask nor did I show a great concern to know at that time. My truth says they were all together wrong because I do want to know and was entitled to know him.

Mothers we must be aware that there are times when children are afraid to ask simple and honest questions of their parents. The question or statement doesn't necessarily make it right to seek an answer from the children but parents must ask themselves why are children seeking others to help them make serious decisions?

Mother's it is not that we have all the solutions or answers for our children's concern alone. I am saying that is it is important for us to be there in their lives seeking out the right answers from qualified others if we don't have them. Don't feel afraid or ashamed to seek out support and assistance from others through counseling, support groups, grandmothers, church, and or friends. It is safe for us to consult one another through social groups to have a pool to select or analyze possible solutions.

My questions seemed to never end; sometimes they just go on and on and on.

As I look back over my life, I have to confess that it really does matter who was my father. It matters because I need to know my heritage.

I have met people who asked me if I knew this person or that person as a relative based on my maiden name (Martin). Darn it! I had to confess painfully each time, "I don't really know." Then, they would ask, "Are you from the Island?" I guess they asked that because when I speak, I speak very fast sometimes, and yes, there is an Islander accent, whatever that is. I just do not know where from. That sounds crazy, huh.

Well there are many children who feel lost or in a zone where they are not connecting. Just like me they know they are from mom for certain but are they not as certain about the other side of their family? What I do not know is my entire heritage. I don't know things like, where did my father's family originate? My birth certificate states that mom came from Arkansas but I have never been there. I guess it is time for a road trip. My birth certificate also says that Dave is from Mississippi. Who knows where Nathan originated?

Just ask somebody, huh. Well my mother needed to know that I wanted to hear it from her. Future mommies and current mommies you have the opportunity to set the record straight now. Tell your children about their fathers.

Due to my embarrassment of not knowing I would make up some story to ease my pain and make it seem like my family was not dysfunctional when asked about my heritage. Yet discovering the truth: we were very much dysfunctional. My, we were like the rest of the world (lol).

No family is perfect but each family member is entitled to one another's love and truth. Who are you sharing your love and truth within your family? Do not be selective about which family member deserves your love or must know the truth because we all deserve to be loved and told the truth.

What Mommy Needed To Know . . .

What Mommy Needed To Know . . .

What Mommy Needed To Know . . .

Who Is My Paternal Family

As mentioned in the previous chapter each time someone asked me about my last name the wound reopens. My mind would wonder into my "Neverland" hoping we were relatives. Heck, there were times I would just settle if we were distant relatives. Even if I opted to pretend that we could have been relatives, I still could not connect the link because I do not know. The truth is this is a pain that lingers.

As an adult I have learned how to accept this fate in my life. Sometimes I tell myself that I am okay because I am all grown-up now. No, it is not okay! I will not continue to play in the melodrama of my mind and say that it is. It is very painful but I am good because I am addressing this concern. How about you? Are you good? Accepting different fates in our lives is essential for survival. You have to determine how you will respond because this guest could show up at your doorstep whether an invitation is given or not. Do you really know your heritage? If you do then I celebrate you.

If you do not know, then ask your parent if he or she is still alive. If your children don't know who is their father, then be sure to tell him or her so they can have the connection and completion in their lives. The old saying "Momma's baby and Daddy's maybe" would be eliminated if someone would just talk about it. Have you heard this before?

Point #4 What mommy needed to know: *Mommy, it matters that you did not share my history because I need to understand where my roots began with not only you. I also am entitled to know about my father and his family. Now that you are gone I feel as though I am deprived of knowing this truth from you or my father.*

Point #4 What future mommies *must* know: *Do not cause your child to suffer undue pain because of a hidden secret of not telling him or her who is their father.*

Children are entitled to know for many reasons their biological father. In fact, this is not about you or the father, but it is about the children. It is not the family's responsibility to tell your children the truth unless you are unable to physically communicate this information.

What Mommy Needed To Know . . .

What Mommy Needed To Know . . .

What Mommy Needed To Know . . .

Will the Real Father Please
Step Up and Be Recognized?

Stepfathers, boyfriends and other men in your life are fine mothers but they do not replace the biological father. It is the right of the children to know, so do not deprive him or her of knowing the truth. There are many men who do not know they have fathered children for various reasons.

Women are ultimately responsible for this initial disconnect. I say women are responsible because women should know their children's father. If you are uncertain, God forbid, regardless be sure to get a blood test immediately. Do not wait until your children are grown to make this introduction. Certainly, this is unfair to everyone.

Mothers, please allow those men to be fathers to their children. Do not be afraid or ashamed of a decision that you made or were forced upon you. I realize some children were conceived through rape, incest, one-night stances, date rape, and there are those who were adopted, along with many other reasons. Yes, these are perhaps painful moments. Nonetheless, truth is still viable and necessary.

Keeping it real from another side and addressing the truth, unfortunately there are times when women use their children as a tool to try to keep control of the children's father. Let him go; however, let him be a father to his children. I am asking you from the children's perspective that did not know how to ask Mommy to explain. I am not indicating that my mother used me as a tool from my father. All I can say in this situation is I don't know what was the major disconnect or even what happened why she never told me.

Next, I am asking you from a woman's perspective that cannot answer her own children's question about their heritage and someone who somewhat repeated the same flaw as my mother. I will share more of this story in my next book. What I will tell you is I didn't get the blood test early with my youngest child so I short-changed his life with his father. Son, I apologize for putting you through that unnecessary pain. Please forgive me. As a mother I am not too proud to ask for my children's forgiveness.

My final suggestion is for you to get the blood test if he denies the children being his when the children are born. Go ahead and match the DNA at birth. Never hold back or be afraid of the truth. The truth really will set you free mentally, spiritually, physically, emotionally, and financially.

Fathers, it is equally your responsibility to step up and make yourself known to your children. You are important and a value-added asset to the children's life and upbringing. Take responsibility for your actions. Your children need you. Be an excellent father for your children, your offspring. Okay, you might have some doubt or even hope that the children are not yours but I challenge you to seek the blood test early on. It is your duty to your children and yourself.

Point #5 What Mommy needed to know: *I was deprived of spending quality time with my biological father and his family. I did not get to play with my cousins or others at the family reunion with daddy's family. You are so important to me. However, addition to you, my father is also part of my genetic make-up. You should have introduced me to him or at least told me about him. I forgive you.*

Point #5 What future mommies *must* know: *It is regardless to how your child was conceived. Tell him or her and help them understand the situation at the appropriate time, hopefully before adulthood. Again, take the necessary test just like you did to find out if you were pregnant. The child is asking you, "Mommy, what are the results? Is he my daddy?*

What Mommy Needed To Know . . .

What Mommy Needed To Know . . .

What Mommy Needed To Know . . .

Who and Where Are the Rest of My Relatives?

So here it starts with repeating a cycle of not really knowing who family is by blood. You know DNA. Have you ever had someone say this is your uncle, aunt, or cousin to later learn that they were really not a blood relative? Does that happen in your family? Now don't misunderstand my point because I know these are great support systems, but they do not replace the truth.

Statistically this is common for the African American family. I believe this is because of how we entered this country as slaves, we were denied the opportunity of knowing who were our people because our men were used to breed children for the slave masters and then literally stripped from their families. They were not allowed for the most part to remain and carry out their duties in their homes as fathers. Slavery no longer exists as it did back then so connect with your family. Fathers stop leaving them alone with their mother to defend and protect. Hey father's she cannot do it alone but she can and most will make it happen to the best of her ability. Our families need you. Yes, the mother is expecting you to be there through the thick and the thin. Your son or daughter is asking, "Daddy, . . . where are you?"

My past statement is not from a blaming or victim mentality but it is the truth as I see and know it. I am not saying this is the truth for all African Americans but I am saying it is for most. Let me caveat that I believe this happens also in other ethnicities and races. As people in general, we are connected as human beings the only true race. Daddy's involvement is good and necessary. Nothing can not replace the truth.

Parents, just tell your children the truth, act like family and keep on moving on. Tell the truth from what you know and not what you imagine or want it to appear. It's known as madness when you don't reveal the truth and live a lie! Oh yeah, some call it drama today when one learns that their adult role model has lied to them for no reason.

The truth doesn't hurt it actually sets you free. If being free "hurts", then the truth does hurt but not in a way to destroy you . . . only to build and take you to the next level. Truth sets you free from the pains of a lie and mistrust permanently. The truth does hurt when you find out after the fact. Lies causes families to break up, stop speaking, and just act real crazy among each other.

Your children are entitled to know what seed they came from in order to understand and breed the proper fruit. Teach and help them understand who they are and not what you want them to become solely. Allow them to be authentic. Coach and encourage them to be who they were originally designed to be.

Remember, God said everything He made was "good". God made your children in His image and likeness. There is greatness inside each of us. Learn to celebrate that greatness. It is my firm belief that whatever we celebrate most is what shows up most. What are you celebrating, thereby giving birth to it? Do not forget it is your responsibility.

Point #6 What mommy needed to know: *Mom, hearing the truth from you is more important than getting it from someone else. Even if you thought it would it hurt me I would have rather gotten it from you so I could have cried in your arms. I loved when you held me in your arms . . . so loving and warm . . . As I tell the truth I can feel you holding me in your arms with love and warmth . . . hum feels really good.*

Point #6 What future mommies *must* know: *The truth builds strong relationship between you and your children so don't be afraid to just "tell them the truth upfront." Don't let anyone else do it for you because it is not someone else responsibility. Remember, others may lie to your children but because they didn't get your story, the truth from you first they won't believe your truth later . . .*

What Mommy Needed To Know . . .

What Mommy Needed To Know . . .

What Mommy Needed To Know . . .

Why Do I Do What I Do and Think The Way I Think?

Sometimes children attempt to behave in matters unbecoming or becoming. This occurs for that matter or whatever the behavior is or appears to be like with a desire to fit in or have a sense of belonging. Yes, you know behaviors that are acceptable or unacceptable to society are what I am referring to. Your home is the first society that your children should role model. Is that society a healthy environment for your seed to be fertilized and grow up in? Children do live what they learn. They must know how to interact with other parts of society without violating another person.

This wanted or unwanted behavior might happen because they don't understand their Chemistry or make up. They do not know their family history on both sides, as far as what is morally or ethically acceptable behavior. Each family develops their own morals and values based on upbringing and socialization.

Everyone has the option of their own choice; however, the choices we often make are based on how we were raised or influenced. Our values and beliefs play an important role in our decision-making process. There are times when individuals have internal ethical conflicts. Conflict is sometimes inevitable when it comes to the decision-making process. It's like, "Why am I doing this or over that?" or "Why do I behave the way I do about certain choices or actions?"

Using fruit as an analogy I will attempt to explain why certain actions may occur. If Mom is an apple and Dad is a pear, you must be prepared for the children to have the personality traits of both mom and dad character. It does not mean one parent's habits or ways are better than the other. One thing for sure is apple trees certainly can't produce a pear. However, we can get a fruit I will call the pear-app if we crossbred the fruits. At that point it is a new tree created with elements from both trees. Yes their roots are from both backgrounds like it or not.

Point #7 What mommy needed to know: *My family trees and ancestry is important in understanding who I am and also for future generations. Mom you didn't share the rest of the fruit tree with me. I don't believe it was the forbidden fruit.*

Point #7 What future mommies *must* know: *Be selective in whom to have children with if you are not prepared to tell your children about their father and his family. Letting your children know their father is about them and not about you. Mother's you must research and understand the background of the possible father prior to conception. I accept this is strong language but it is essential information. For example, if mom has Sickle Cell or the trait and she mates with a man who likewise have the trait it is more than likely the child will have the disease. Harvard education notes,*

> Sickle cell disease is an inherited condition. Two genes for the sickle hemoglobin must be inherited from one's parents in order to have the disease. A person who receives a gene for sickle cell disease from one parent and a normal gene from the other has a condition called "sickle cell trait". Sickle cell trait produces no symptoms or problems for most people. Sickle cell disease can neither be contracted nor passed on to another person. The severity of sickle cell disease varies tremendously. Some people with sickle cell disease lead lives that are nearly normal. Others are less fortunate, and can suffer from a variety of complications.

What Mommy Needed To Know . . .

What Mommy Needed To Know . . .

What Mommy Needed To Know . . .

Part II

What Mommy Needed To Know . . .

Clarity Starts Here for Me

Basically, I never questioned Mother about who my father was despite knowing that my stepfather was not my biological father. I guess it really didn't matter at the time to seek out my natural father because I had a father image in my life. It was like some forbidden thing in my mind to ask her about him. That was easy for me to do because we just didn't talk about it in our home.

I guess because she never talked about him, I really did not think about him. Yet the truth is, it really did and does matter about my father. When I was a child I thought like a child but now that I am an adult I put away childish things and think like an adult.

How would children seek out their father or is this even possible when they are minors? So, I did what any children would do and that is accept the man mother had placed in my life.

Some might say Bradley, my stepfather who I called daddy, wasn't the greatest father but I will say he was there. As I write and ask questions of others I am learning more about my mother and her husband. I learned that my mother had really endured a lot. Mommy, in actuality intended to take care and provide the best for her children despite any odds. Thanks mommy.

You know, I didn't even realize the pain and challenges my mother faced until I heard it from others who knew them. Good mothers protect their children in all situations and against all odds based on their capability. My mother did a good job raising her children despite the pains life brought.

My mom put our welfare and needs before her own. Real mothers sacrifice for their children they don't bring harm to them. Future mommies get help if you feel as though you can't take it any more. Your children are vulnerable and really look to you for their safety. Don't betray their trust in you. Never quit or give up on yourself or your children. They don't ask nor deserve to be abused, rejected, murdered by your hands or anyone else. Yes, this is strong language but I must be the one to speak out on their behalf. I can hear my mother telling me to tell you this truth. I tell you this truth because I love humankind. Guess what that means I love you because you are humankind.

I was very much content with the family I had at that time, my mother my stepfather and my two sisters. Truth of the matter is I really did not have a choice in the matter. I did, however, trust my mother's decisions. Remember, none of us chose what family we are born in. Also we don't know why, when, and who would be in our lineage or have control where they come from. It is the responsibility of the parent concerning those choices. Yes, you chose who your children are connected to by blood in this life here on earth.

Point #8 What mommy needed to know: *I believe you made the best choice possible for my sisters and me to the best of your ability. Thank you for the sacrifices you made for us. I could sense something was happening after you got sick. There were a lot of changes and not for the good of everyone. I didn't understand the pain you were experiencing. I love you for not giving up on my sisters and me.*

Point #8 What future mommies *must* know: *Your children trust you to make the best decisions for their lives. You are their heroine for life. So do your best at being your best for them and yourself. You don't have to settle for being less than a mother to them. Get help if you need a break. Mothers are entitled to a break sometimes (smile). When you check out for that break, let me encourage you to check back in better than you where when you checked out.*

What Mommy Needed To Know . . .

What Mommy Needed To Know . . .

What Mommy Needed To Know . . .

The Middle-Child Syndrome

One thing I know for certain is that I am the middle child of my mother's three living children. I have two sisters, Natashae, my oldest and Irene, my youngest sister. Sisters I love you. Thanks for being there as we grew up even though you did put the pillow over my head a couple of times out of play. I forgive you sisters. I love you. You are the greatest Sisters in the whole world. I was told that I had a brother who was stillborn or mother miscarried. I don't know because I don't recall her discussing it with me. What I do know is I love my sisters and we had fun growing up with our mother.

There were times when I felt unsure of my family's love. I think this was because I am the middle child. My eldest sister clung to mom and my youngest was close to her father, my stepfather. There were times when I just felt alone and it was I all by myself.

Trust me, there is some truth to the birth order of children. If you haven't researched the birth order, I encourage and invite you to do so—it is no longer a secret. In fact, I am going to share some statistics with you from a known psychologist.

Psychologist Kevin Leman (2002) shared advice for parents on what to expect from their children depending on their birth order while being a guest on *The Early Show*. He advised,

> "These kids are the most difficult to pin down. They are guaranteed to be opposite of their older sibling, but that difference can manifest in a variety of ways. Middle children often feel like their older brother gets all the glory while their younger sister escapes all discipline. Because the middle child feels that the world pays him less attention, he tends to be secretive; he does not openly share his thoughts or feelings. That the middle children may not feel they have a special place in the family so friends and peer groups become

much more important. They can usually read people well, they are peacemakers who see all sides of a situation, they are independent and inventive."

His observation actually proved true for my personality. It's very interesting how studies conducted have value to them. Expand your knowledge by learning more about yourself and your children. Reading is truly more than fundamental. It is another opportunity to develop one's knowledge base.

Point #9 What mommy needed to know: *I know you knew me but not enough to know how I was truly feeling inside. Or you were in denial because you didn't know how to help me. I understand I was only eleven years old when you died and you had so much on your mind. I am certain that our spirits deeply connected but I really know in my heart that our love ran deeper than any ocean.*

Point #9 What future mommies *must* know: *Learn the birth order effect, study your children but most importantly understand who you are so you can help your children. Get to know the spirit on the inside of not only them but also yourself. Spirit does relate to spirit. How deep does your love go, how wide and how long does it go for your children?*

What Mommy Needed To Know . . .

What Mommy Needed To Know . . .

What Mommy Needed To Know . . .

Mom's Homegrown Cooking

Ultimately, as I was growing up it really didn't matter much about who was my father because I truly loved my mother and her great cooking, as Campbell Soup says, "um um good".

I can remember there being a beautiful garden filled with vegetables in our backyard that our mother tended to and harvested for us to eat. Every year the earth gave us new and fresh vegetables. I believe we grew greens, cabbage, tomatoes, and other vegetables. I used to love the stewed tomatoes, greens, black-eyed peas, sweet potatoes, cornbread, and other foods she prepared for us. Mother also went to the fields and local markets to get vegetables and fruits for her family.

I recall mother eating a lot of beets. Ugh, when I was a little girl I did not like beets. Now in my adult life, beets are one of my favorite vegetables. Food from Mommy's garden was yummy for my tummy.

Vegetables are a great source of nutrition. My mother ensured that I had vegetables with every meal. When I was growing up microwaves weren't invented or we didn't have one in our homes. I loved the smell of good cooking coming from the stove. Gosh, my mom worked and still cooked healthy meals for her family. Thanks Mom for feeding me.

Point #10 What mommy needed to know: *I enjoyed your cooking. I miss eating your food. You were a great provider. Our foods were very healthy for us. Mother you were a wonderful cook.*

Point #10 What future mommies *must* know: *Take time to prepare your children a healthy and wholesome meal. If you work prepare it early, freeze it and let them eat a microwave plate that you prepared. Your family will appreciate it. Children really prefer to eat your healthy food instead of a fast food meal that has no nutrients or a dish from your local grocery frozen food section you throw in the microwave if raised this way from early childhood.*

What Mommy Needed To Know . . .

What Mommy Needed To Know . . .

What Mommy Needed To Know . . .

Pets are for Keeps and They Bring Balance

During my early childhood life I grew up with Butch, our dog, and Missy, our cat. I don't quite remember when we got these animals as pets but I do remember the love I had for them. It was our responsibility to feed them and take care of them. I use to play with Butch in our yard. He was such a great pet and a wonderful watch dog. He had a beautiful heart. You could see it in his eyes. There was something special about having pets as a part of the family. One of my sister's swore that Missy was a boy, but I could have sworn she was a girl cat. Actually the gender did not matter because I loved our pets!

Winters were sometimes cold and harsh in Benton Harbor. I recall one cold winter we accidentally locked our cat outside and she froze to death. As a young girl I, of course, was very sad to lose our cat. We gave our cat a funeral and buried it in mother's garden. Our garden became Missy's new permanent home. We had our own pet cemetery right out back behind the house.

Interestingly enough after burying and missing her for a few days, we continued to play as little girls. Isn't that how life is so supposed to be? Yes, we mustn't die but we must choose to live given any circumstance or situation.

I know losing a pet is nowhere the same as losing a person for some; however, grief is just that grief. Who or what are you still grieving? I respect the fact that you are grieving; however, I hope to strengthen you to not get stuck.

Once the loved one is buried, we have to move on with life and not stay stuck. That's what I believe they would want for us once we properly grieve. No one can really say how long the process may take for you. All I encourage you to do is not become overcome by grief and stop living.

Pets can be therapeutic for any household. So if your child wants a pet, may I suggest that you do not deprive him or her of this responsibility? I encourage you to find and negotiate a way to teach them how to handle responsibilities early on by allowing some kind of pet. Pets are family members.

In fact, there is a lot of study and documentation developed addressing how therapeutic dogs have been for human beings. Dogs have been used to assist the blind or even to let a person know if they are getting ready to experience a seizure or other health challenges. The bottom line is most pets just have a loving and caring spirit about them.

Now as I stated, pets do come with responsibilities but they generally can survive when they don't get attention better than a human being. Children sometimes find security by having a pet to share their love, teach responsibility, assist in healing properties, share a meal under the table, or help them learn discipline through responsibilities.

Unfortunately, sometimes there are some people who treat their pets better than their children. Don't mistake what I am saying by taking it out of context thinking it is okay to love your pet more than your children because I am not. I am saying we can learn things from the animal kingdom that would positively certainly serve our human kingdom.

Being brought up with pets has aided me in not only becoming a huge pet lover, but having that responsibility helped me be more responsible as I clearly understood there is a proper place and time for the right thing to be done all the time. Of course there is definitely more for me to learn but having Butch and Missy was a positive thing in my life as a child.

Point #11 What mommy needed to know: *I had an authentic and genuine love not only for you but for our pets as well. Losing Missy somewhat prepared me to know how to grieve when I lost something and someone very close to me. Interestingly, it probably assisted me subconsciously when the greater lost occurred in my life at eleven. Oh yeah, in case you did not know, Missy was buried in the garden.*

Point #11 What future mommies *must* know: *Children have an authentic and genuine love for you. When given the opportunity to own a pet their love for the pets are also authentic. Understand when they lose a pet to death or the fish has to be dumped in the toilet and they cry they will get over it shortly. Be patient through the grieving process of their loss. We all grieve differently so respect and be compassionate when someone is grieving a loss.*

What Mommy Needed To Know . . .

What Mommy Needed To Know . . .

What Mommy Needed To Know . . .

Balance Yes, That's What It's Called

Is your life balanced? Too often as mothers we become imbalanced trying to juggle this and that at the same time. I know it has been said women are better multi-taskers than men. Actually there is some truth to this saying. Multitasking can also be detrimental to other family members and mom, alike. Over tasking can lead to breakdowns.

Most women are wired or have been trained to handle more than one thing at a time. She takes care of the children, cook the food, work a full time job, assist with home, clean the house, and so much more, not to mention her man if he is a part of the household. Unfortunately, being imbalanced has cost many women their sanity. It has placed such a burden on the family. Families can no longer be at risk and become well known on the list of extinction.

Men I am asking and seeking you to help mothers balance life with the children. Mothers who are imbalanced have placed their children at risk. The home is a place of safety, a place of love a place of laughter and where problem solving can occur ethically. Nonetheless, as a result of imbalance it is becoming a place of tragedy.

Mother's balance is very important. It is a criteria that should be implemented when making a decision that affects the lives of others and hers as well. Everyone should understand how to properly balance life responsibly. We will process balance or lack of balance more in-depth in one of my next books.

Point #12 What mommy needed to know: *I learned how to balance and juggle things in life because I watched you. Again, I am honored to credit you for helping me adapt to life during your short span here on earth. I have been able to achieve and accomplish much because of this teaching. However, when I don't plan properly I have crashed at things I should have succeeded. I still hear your still voice guiding me saying, "Stay humble, be determined to win, yet stay balanced."*

Point #12 What future mommies *must* know: *Showing your children how to balance life so they can make valuable decisions is your responsibility and it is very important. Balance actually creates an environment for growth to occur. It can lessen confusion when things appear chaotic. Balance is associated with priority, order and stability.*

What Mommy Needed To Know . . .

What Mommy Needed To Know . . .

What Mommy Needed To Know . . .

Neighbors and Friends are Just Like Family

A significant neighbor that I remember and want to mention in this book is Ms. Ethel Davis. She was a friend, a neighbor of our family, and a member of our church. We attended Honorable Door Baptist Church on Main Street in Benton Harbor.

Ms. Davis is remembered in my book for the homemade ice cream she shared every winter with my sisters and me. I can recall eating some of the best ice cream and it seemed like the worlds best to me. Our ice cream came from the rooftop of our houses. I used to love when it snowed.

When the first snowfall came, Ms. Davis sent one of her grandsons—John, Jonathan, or Daniel—to the top of the roof during the winter months to collect snow so she could make us fresh homemade ice cream. Wow, that ice cream was really tasty. I always got excited when it snowed because I knew I would have homemade ice cream. When we moved from our house, it was sad because there was no more homemade ice cream for me to eat. Last I heard was Ms. Davis is now deceased, and I have no idea where her grandsons are living today. Even though she is no longer physically in my life she made a huge impact on me. She gave more than homemade ice cream. She fed my soul spiritually.

Point #13 What mommy needed to know: *I enjoyed living in our home. I was so content and spent some of the best years of my life on Urbandale Street. Thanks Mommy for giving me a "home." I know you knew that I loved the homemade ice cream Ms. Davis made for me. Mom thanks for letting me have a healthy dessert.*

Point #13 What future mommies *must* know: *Your child deserves a safe, loving home and you are responsible for providing it. Our neighbors are important people to know. Make the time to know who is in your neighborhood. Not all neighbors are bad but it is your responsibility to know who are the bad ones. The real only way to sort them out is get to know them. Its okay to take on southern hospitality for sake of protecting your environment. Healthy sweets are good once in a while. In fact, take the time to share a healthy treat with your children today after dinner. I promise they won't forget.*

What Mommy Needed To Know . . .

What Mommy Needed To Know . . .

What Mommy Needed To Know . . .

Life at Honorable Door Baptist Church

I can recall every Sunday, mother and my stepfather would ensure I went to church. I was in church when the doors opened and when they closed. I did not complain because I really loved Sunday school and attending Baptist Training Union, commonly known as BTU in the Baptist Church. Besides, I was a kid with not much choice in the matter. There was no problem with me attending because Ms. Davis was my BTU teacher, remember she also made me homemade ice-cream. She was a great lady.

One of my favorite things was the Bible drill at BTU. Wow, did I love and enjoy participating in these drills. I can hear the leader even now saying to others and me as we stood there, "Draw Sword" (which meant get your Bible in your hand with your hand on top of it). They would say the Bible verse, and then we anxiously waited to hear "Charge!" That meant "Go, go, go" the first one to find the scripture and start reading the verse from the Bible won! Not only did someone win but, recognition was always given for everyone's efforts. Just thinking about those days brings a smile to my face. I really did love going to church.

Point #14 What mommy needed to know: *I appreciate you not only for taking me to church but also involving me in a church that supported my growth and learning.*

Point #14 What future mommies *must* know: *Your children needs a church or spiritual environment, which supports you and them. This place must reinforce your value system as it instills growth and learning. You must know who is training your children so, go along with them and get involved. It's your responsibility and not the church alone. Make sure they are teaching what you want your children to learn according to your belief and value system.*

What Mommy Needed To Know . . .

What Mommy Needed To Know . . .

What Mommy Needed To Know . . .

Our Church is Our Community

The church that set back on the Main Street became my second home. We went to our second home routinely every Sunday without fail. My stepfather was the superintendent of the Sunday school and I actually earned the opportunity of becoming the secretary.

Becoming the Sunday school's secretary really enhanced my administrative skills. Later in my life I typed sermons which aided in me in becoming a phenomenal typist for another church I attended. I know this is where my strong development and foundation began spiritually. Yes, the church was important and assisted me in finding the strength I needed to survive as a child becoming an adult. Believe it or not, this is what got me through the challenges I faced throughout my life.

There are many skills, which children learn at an early age they apply when they are older. Children should experience a life that builds a strong foundation. This foundation is designed to assist them on how to deal with challenges, how to feel the fear and do it anyway and foremost how to never give up. Children must observe winners right in their homes. Are you your children's heroine or hero? You go she-ro. I salute you because you are a winner, a winner indeed in the lives of your seed.

Mothers, you must connect spiritually with your Creator. It is the Creator who will teach you how to raise your children. In order to understand malfunction or how to properly raise them you have to consult their Creator. For me God is the Creator of All. The Creator is Supreme.

Point #15 What mommy needed to know: *I am so grateful. Thanks Mom, if I never told you how much I appreciated you for giving me this gift of life and love through a nurturing and caring church community. Watching you work in the church made me proud of you. It actually gave me a sense of belonging and encouraged me to get involved. You are and will always be my heroine and she-ro for life. I shared these same principles and values with my children.*

Point #15 What future mommies *must* know: *You are responsible for training your children, providing spiritual guidance, and ensuring they have a secure foundation. You do not have to do this alone. Find a church or spiritual relationship. Become a part of one that meets the needs of your entire family. This can be an intricate and positive part of your child's adult process. This can also provide a great social support system for you. You must get your children involved in the spiritual process. Allow and encourage them to participate in programs. This process will assist in shaping their future.*

What Mommy Needed To Know . . .

What Mommy Needed To Know . . .

What Mommy Needed To Know . . .

The Move That Changed My Life as a Little Girl

When I was either nine or ten years old we moved into our new house on Highland Avenue in Benton Harbor because Mother became sicker. Little I know but she had cancer. This time, this home felt different because I could feel the change in the atmosphere. Our family wasn't the same.

My mom was very sick so she could not work. I think my stepfather worked, but I also believe other things were going on that I didn't understand in our home nor was it explained. All I know is we lost our house on Urbandale Street due to lack of funds is what my eldest sister told me. Foreclosure is not something new in the twenty-first century—it existed way before then. We do need an honest bailout to preserve not only the housing industry, but the family who made the house a "home." It is my prayer that the people in charge begin to show true compassion for the lay people. I am not advocating a government run society but I am advocating a partnership between the government and the people for all people. The center of our compass must become our children worldwide for the sake of the earth.

Our dog, Butch, moved to Highland Avenue with us. His new home became the backyard, unlike having privileges both inside our home on Urbandale Street. I do not know what happened but we were not your usual girls because we started feeding our dog gunpowder after we moved. I do not recall us ever doing that in the past. The reason why I mentioned this is because children will often do silly things and not understand why. Despite our juvenile acts mother loved us unconditionally. Unconditional love requires work and it can happen. Many people practice it everyday.

Okay, animal rights individuals, don't come and arrest us. We were just silly little girls who meant no harm. I guess we're having fun and thought it was a good idea. I really can't answer why we fed him gunpowder with his food, but I do know he was a great protector. You know, Butch never became sick. He was a great buddy. Thanks, Mom, for ensuring we had pets.

Mothers as I mentioned before your children can learn personal responsibilities with pets. You can teach them how to by sharing a pet if you can afford it. If you cannot afford the pet or the possibility of pet abuse then seek another responsibility lesson. They can learn responsibility through keeping their room clean, taking out the trash, or simply washing dishes with you. Make this quality and fun times not just chores.

Point #16 What mommy needed to know: *I love you for giving our home a pet. It helped with our unforeseen move. Thanks for being open-minded and understanding the psychology behind having pets in the home (even though Butch and Missy were indoor/outdoor pets). Thanks for giving me the opportunity to learn responsibility.*

Point #16 What future mommies *must* know: *If your child does not have a pet for whatever reason, make time to stop at the local pet store or humane society. Pets are therapeutic. Moving from one place to another can be traumatic for children. Even though you attempt to make it as smooth or simple as possible. Teach your children about chores as you teach and train them by allowing it to be seen as quality time between you and them.*

What Mommy Needed To Know . . .

What Mommy Needed To Know . . .

What Mommy Needed To Know . . .

The Fastest Walk of My Young Life

Another story that I have selected to share in this book is when I remember being in the third grade at Cooley Elementary School in Benton Harbor. My third-grade teacher used to ball up a paper and put it in my bosom. You know, inside of my blouse. To this day I have no idea why she did that to me. Well, one day I decided to tell my mother what was happening to me because I did not understand nor like it.

I do not remember if we had a car at that time; Mother was not driving or my stepfather was gone with the car. I do know my mom and I walked at least one mile to the school to talk to the teacher. Whew, we had to walk a true country mile to the school for my mother to confront the teacher. Figuratively, it was like walking several blocks in Chicago or a big city. I was tired but I knew I had to get there with Mom. Geez, I was so tired.

"Come on, Shirley Ann, keep up," I can hear her saying. Her stride also let me know that she was determined that her little girl was not going to be abused, misused, or taken advantage of. She wanted to show me, regardless of her being sick, she would still take care of me. Mother had a spirit of determination. She had willpower that did not include quitting. She was a strong and powerful woman.

Mother was a fast walker so I had to walk fast to keep up with her. Faster and faster our steps moved. It seemed that our steps were moving at the pace of being in a car. Her faced was fixed with not only the willpower to make it to the school but with unction of making this right for her baby girl. It was good exercise even back then. By golly, I believe Mom taught me how to "power walk"! I believe this is why I walk fast today.

My heart pounded faster and faster because I was afraid of the outcome. Man, I didn't want to get in trouble. Oh my goodness we are at the school. What am I going to do? What would I say to Mother? Will the teacher lie and say she does not know what I am talking about?

Well, I became more afraid of the teacher. I lied and told my mother I hadn't told her the truth after we arrived to the school and had met with my teacher. My mom gave me this strange look and the next sound I heard was *whop!* My mother smacked me in my mouth and told me to never lie to her. She promised while assuring me that she was there to support me. Her actions were always to ensure that my sisters and I was taken care of. I felt embarrassed and humiliated.

Even though I was humiliated and embarrassed I was more hurt because I didn't trust my mother. However, what my mother didn't know is I didn't know how to talk with her. I had a secret that I was hiding from her. You will learn about this secret in the upcoming chapter. I will share why I had became afraid to be open with mom. Actually, I did trust her but it's probably better to say I didn't know how to tell her how I was feeling.

My mother was probably disappointed that I had embarrassed her. She probably also knew the truth but she couldn't defend me because I changed my story. One thing for sure is my mother did not curse out the teacher nor did she conduct herself in a manner to further embarrass her or me. Even though mother smacked me in my mouth she didn't commit child abuse in my mind. She did instill the fear of God in me because there was something else I needed to tell her but didn't know how.

Mother taught me the true value of telling the truth. Mothers must realize this is an accountability issue between them and their children. Mommies take the time to explain your actions to your children when necessary. This action does not take away your power as a mother but it is a great opportunity to mentor your children. I learned and grew from this value interaction between Mother and me. After all, my mother was sick and had walked a great distance to go the mile for me, her daughter. Yes, she did it for me, Shirley Ann. What extra steps are you doing to assist your children learn valuable life lessons, even if you don't feel like it because you are sick or dying?

Point #17 What mommy needed to know: *I apologize for embarrassing you. I changed my story because I was afraid, but I actually told you the truth. I respected and loved you but I had another secret happening in my life that impacted me from telling you the truth. So I chose the lesser of the two evils.*

Point #17 What future mommies *must* know: *Teachers have an influence on your children. Ensure you spend time at the school and also know what is going on in your children's life daily.*

Even now as I write this, my eyes swell up in tears because it hurts that I didn't know how to share what I was truly feeling with my mother. I knew my mother loved me and wanted only the best for me but I had failed her. How I wished I could have expressed myself to my mom. I had kept the truth from the woman who gave me life and who genuinely loved me. I found myself caught in a tough decision.

My teacher actually lied to my mother because she was actually guilty of committing an inappropriate act against me. Teachers are supposed to offer the truth and solutions. My teacher did not offer my mother the truth or a solution to make the matter better. On the other hand, I had lied to mom by not telling her the truth because I was afraid. I lied out of fear.

Parents must be aware that not all teachers tell the truth or take actions against children that are always healthy. While I know this also is not absolutely the standard for all teachers, it is important for parents and teachers to work together for the betterment of the children. When either adult do not take the best appropriate action for the children confusion lies in the midst.

Even though my mother told me I did not have to lie to her many times, I found myself lying. Oh my goodness, things were falling apart for this little girl. I told mom the truth but I became confused and more afraid of the consequences from the teacher than my mother so I changed my story. The power and influence of a teacher over a confused student can be dangerous.

Teachers spend a lot of time with children on a daily basis. Sometimes they spend more time with children than parents do. My caution to parents is to get involved and stay involved. Be seen in the schools, volunteer when possible and let your phone number be known to the teacher.

I reiterated the incident with the teacher because it is important for parents to stay involved. Remember we discussed earlier about you being first in line when it comes to the welfare of your children. As the old saying goes, "the squeaky wheel gets the oil". Finally let me encourage you to attend parent teacher conferences and school board meetings. These are your children and the school system is not responsible for raising your children. Be involved. It's another way to show love for your children.

After everything was over and we left the school, my dear mother explained why I should always tell her the truth. So many different thoughts ran through my head as she talked to me. My little negative voice started to talk to me offering different ideas further confusing the situation. I was probably half-listening to what my mother was saying because of the confusion happening in my head.

Has your mind ever raced with unnecessary and unfruitful thoughts that bombarded you? In some kind of way, I think I stilled heard mom. Yes mother's voice was very prominent. A mother's voice is always ringing in her children's ear. Children remember what their mother taught them. Oh yeah, what about the look. No one could give you the eye and have the supersonic ears like mother. She is truly a gift from God to her children.

I was not mad at my mother, neither was I disappointed by her actions. The worst thing happened at that time because I became withdrawn and afraid was I left my mother speechless. I felt as though Mother had lost trust in me. The worst thing for this little girl was she "lied" to her mother about something very true and real after telling her the truth at first.

Point #18 What mommy needed to know: *Mother, I am asking you to please forgive me for lying to you and not developing an honest, open, and willing mother-and-daughter relationship. I truly was afraid. I had a dilemma but didn't know how to handle it. I gave you a situation to handle for me then I took it back. I am sorry. Thanks for forgiving me. I can hear your forgiveness resonating throughout my entire being.*

Point #18 What future mommies *must* know: *Your children's thinking capacity is not what they think when it comes to reasoning. They will and can become confused because their brain isn't fully developed when it comes to making rational decisions (checkout "Development Across the Life Span" by Robert S. Feldman along with other documentation sharing about cognitive development). Times will come unfortunately when your precious children become afraid and they allow the circumstances circumvent the love you have for them. I encourage to further build a relationship where they can tell you the truth no matter what, as you understand their growth process.*

What Mommy Needed To Know . . .

What Mommy Needed To Know . . .

What Mommy Needed To Know . . .

Sometimes Children Lie to Spare the Family Pain

F or the sake of continuing to spare the family more pain I am changing his name to Mr. Bad Guy as I tell you about a horrible thing that happened to me as a little girl. I used to see him after I got out of school. Goodness I just in the third grade. Mom felt it was okay for me to go to their home because his wife would cook sometimes for us and was a nice lady. His daughter and my eldest sister were friends.

Well, Mr. Bad used to take me for a ride in his car. He would have me sit on his lap so I could be tall enough to see over the windowsill to drive, or so I thought. I do not want to be totally graphic in this book; however, if you would use your imagination on what happened to me, it happened.

Yes, you guessed it! This old man took my virginity. It's pretty painful to think about it even now. It happens unfortunately every day, somewhere to some child.

In all fairness my Mother did not know because I did not tell her or anyone else. I was fascinated that I could drive a car at a young age. Dang it! He not only molested but he raped me. Yes, this impacted my life drastically because I did not understand what had happened to me. The sad part before this book I didn't tell anyone what had happened to me until some twenty years later.

What you will find next are statistics validating what happened to me happens to children on a daily basis. These facts are overwhelming, they happen too often, and are alarming. Statistics surrounding the issue of child sexual abuse document how sex offenders abuse children. In presenting the statistics, the pages are organized by Prevalence and Consequences. They are also validated by the National Crimes of Victims.

The statistics from Darkness2Light are shocking:

   ☐   1 in 4 girls is sexually abused before the age of 18.

- 1 in 6 boys is sexually abused before the age of 18.
- 1 in 5 children is solicited sexually while on the Internet.
- Nearly 70% of all reported sexual assaults (including assaults on adults) occur to children ages 17 and under.
- An estimated 39 million survivors of childhood sexual abuse exist in America today.

Even within the walls of their own homes, children are at risk for sexual abuse

- 30-40% of victims are abused by a family member.
- Another 50% are abused by someone outside of the family whom they know and Trust.
- Approximately 40% are abused by older or larger children whom they know.
- Therefore, only 10% are abused by strangers.

Sexual abuse can occur at all ages, probably younger than you think

- The median age for reported abuse is 9 years old.
- More than 20% of children are sexually abused before the age of 8.
- Nearly 50% of all victims of forcible sodomy, sexual assault with an object, and forcible fondling are children under 12.

Most children don't tell even if they have been asked

- Evidence that a child has been sexually abused is not always obvious, and many children do not report that they have been abused.
- Over 30% of victims never disclose the experience to *anyone*.
- Young victims may not recognize their victimization as sexual abuse.
- Almost 80% initially deny abuse or are tentative in disclosing. Of those who do disclose, approximately 75% disclose accidentally. Additionally, of those who do disclose, more than 20% eventually recant even though the abuse occurred.
- Fabricated sexual abuse reports constitute only 1-4% of all reported cases. Of these reports, 75% are falsely reported by adults and 25% are reported by children. children only fabricate 0.5% of the time.

Consequences of child sexual abuse begin affecting children and families immediately. They also affect society in innumerable and negative ways. These effects can continue throughout the life of the survivor so the impact on society for just one survivor continues over multiple decades. Try to imagine the impact of thirty-nine million survivors.

Health and/or Behavioral Problems:

- [ ] The way a victim's family responds to abuse plays an important role in how the incident affects the victim.
- [ ] Sexually abused children who keep it a secret or who "tell" and are not believed are at greater risk than the general population for psychological, emotional, social, and physical problems often lasting into adulthood.
- [ ] children who have been victims of sexual abuse are more likely to experience physical health problems (e.g., headaches).
- [ ] Victims of child sexual abuse report more symptoms of PTSD, sadness, and school problems than nonvictims. (10, 16, 55, 72)
- [ ] Victims of child sexual abuse are more likely to experience major depressive disorders as adults. (55, 72)
- [ ] Young girls who are sexually abused are more likely to develop eating disorders as adolescents. (16, 40, 89)
- [ ] Adolescent victims of violent crime have difficulty in the transition to adulthood, are more likely to suffer financial failure and physical injury, and are at risk to fail in other areas due to problem behaviors and outcomes of the victimization.

Drug and/or Alcohol Problems:

- [ ] Victims of child sexual abuse report more substance abuse problems. 70-80% of sexual abuse survivors report excessive drug and alcohol use. (10, 16, 89)
- [ ] Young girls who are sexually abused are 3 times more likely to develop psychiatric disorders or alcohol and drug abuse in adulthood, than girls who are not sexually abused. (16, 40, 89)
- [ ] Among male survivors, more than 70% seek psychological treatment for issues such as substance abuse, suicidal thoughts and attempted suicide. Males who have been sexually abused are more likely to violently victimize others. (90)

Teenage Pregnancy and Promiscuity:

- [ ] Children who have been victims of sexual abuse exhibit long-term and more frequent behavioral problems, particularly inappropriate sexual behaviors.

☐ Women who report childhood rape are three times more likely to become pregnant before age 18.

☐ An estimated 60% of teen first pregnancies are preceded by experiences of molestation, rape, or attempted rape. The average age of their offenders is 27 years old.

☐ Victims of child sexual abuse are more likely to be sexually promiscuous. (39, 59, 60, 70)

☐ More than 75% of teenage prostitutes have been sexually abused.

Crime:

☐ Adolescents who suffer violent victimization are at risk for being victims or perpetrators of felony assault, domestic violence, and property offense as adults.

☐ Nearly 50% of women in prison state that they were abused as children.

☐ Over 75% of serial rapists report they were sexually abused as youngsters.

Most perpetrators don't molest only one child if they are not reported and stopped

☐ Nearly 70% of child sex offenders have between 1 and 9 victims; at least 20% have 10 to 40 victims. (23)

☐ An average serial child molester may have as many as 400 victims in his lifetime.

It is interesting that these stats seem unreal but they are very much real in our society. These are not worldwide stats but sadly US stats. It is time for us to keep our children safe from unstable individuals. Can you imagine the number of rapes and molestation cases like my unfortunate experience that have never been reported? Unfortunately, I never reported what happened to me. I am asking young people and responsible adults, begging you to not allow what happened to me happen to you or your children.

I never told my Mother. I put up a front like everything was fine but I was living a lie again out of fear. I also wanted to keep driving that car, such a silly little girl. Yes, a little girl who had no idea what was happening to her but also threatened if I told. Heck, my third grade teacher lied and didn't tell the truth, certainly Mr. Bad would do the same.

Oprah Winfrey just conducted a program (November 5, 2010) on the Oprah Show where 200 men took courage and addressed their past childhood filled with molestation. This is indisputable and unacceptable. Everyone was impacted because of some sick adult's decision to abuse a child. I empathize with the victims. Yet I salute you for your bravery and ability to seek help. Thanks Tyler for leading from the front and also being a spokesperson regardless to your social status. I felt the pain of the men in the room. I pray your family members understand and stand by you as you heal from this drastic tragedy.

Point #19 What mommy needed to know: *I needed your protection from people who could hurt me. I know I should have let you known so you could protect me but I was afraid. I did not know how to tell you I was being molested. I am sorry. I also knew you were sick and didn't want to add to the problems at home. You would have killed him and went to jail.*

Point #19 What future mommies *must* know: *Your sons and daughters want you to protect them from people who can hurt them. Be open and willing to listen to your child. I can't tell you how you would know if they don't tell you what's happening but Lord knows I pray you find out. Whenever, you find out take the appropriate action. My Mom never got that opportunity because I didn't tell her.*

The situation of being violated really impacted who I was becoming. It affected my self-esteem as well as my mindset about life. It drastically impacted my development as I was becoming the little girl who was about to lose her mother for life. So many issues happening all at once for a little girl or boy to handle can be devastating.

Parents you must be involved in your children's lives. Please don't trust a system or someone else to properly do your job. I am not implying that my Mother relied on a system because she didn't know. I threw the detour in her agenda for saving her little girl from what I called embarrassment or torture. Actually as I think about it, I believe Mother would have murdered this man for violating her little girl.

Point #20 What mommy needed to know: *I lost my virginity as a little girl (around age 10ish) and it was not my choice. I was violated unfairly. I missed the opportunity of growing up with you helping me through this crisis because I didn't know how to tell you. I put your sickness before my welfare. Mom, I don't blame you for not being there because I never told you.*

Point #20 What future mommies *must* know: *Your sons and daughters need you to assist them with their crisis. Watch for behavioral changes, talk with them and let them know they won't get in trouble for telling you the truth. One significant point is "You" must be healed in order to properly help them heal. Quality relationships with your children don't instantly happen but it requires constant work. What you must know and accept is they can be formed for life.*

What Mommy Needed To Know . . .

What Mommy Needed To Know . . .

What Mommy Needed To Know . . .

This Sickness Was unto Death

Well, despite Mom's health challenges, we continued our routine of going to church and being a loving family, as we knew it when possible. She was diagnosed with the awful disease of cancer. Mother was very prayerful and faithful in believing for her healing. It is my belief that she really was more concerned about what would happen to her girls after she left this earth more than anything else. Mother never really let us, or should I say me, in on her real pain. I believe her heart was broken and this would become her final fate in life. She was only about thirty-seven years old when she left us. She was younger than that when she became ill. Cancer attacked her body very fast.

I do not ever recall her complaining other than her being in pain. I never really understood what was happening. We didn't talk much about her sickness. I know she was in and out of the hospital. Mommy was very young when she left this earth to never return to her little girls. Yes, her sickness was unto death.

Mothers are so important to their children. Nothing stayed the same after mother became very ill. Our entire lives were changed and definitely not for the better. She was crippled to the point where she could not do for us as she had in the past. I could sense that our family was falling apart. One of the things I recognized was mother was the key in our family. She loved her girls more than anything and we loved her.

Point #21 What mommy needed to know: *I knew you were in pain. Actually it hurt to have not been able to help you. I thought I was helping you when I did not share how I was feeling knowing you would be leaving me. I still hurt because I don't have you in my life. I miss you Mommy.*

Point #21 What future mommies *must* know: *Your child can feel your pain. He or she may not understand it but because they came from your womb they are linked to you. It is important to share major challenges with your children so they do not have to seek answers from someone else.*

Death showed up and took mother with it

Our mom became more ill with the ugly disease of cancer. I didn't really understand what all that meant but I knew Mommy was different. I wish Tahitian Noni Bioactive Beverage could have been discovered back then in the United States; perhaps it could have helped her. I say this because I know this product has helped so many others. There are human clinical trials showing this product does fight free radicals. Take the time to find out about this gift from God as referred to by the French Polynesians (*www.tni. com/2496331*).

After moving from our home on Urbandale Ms. Queen Lady, our pastor's wife and Mother's friend became very active in our family. Her involvement was probably because she knew just how sick Mother had become. She was not only the First Lady of our church but she was a prayer warrior. I can recall when we used to go to her home for prayer meetings.

Those prayer meetings were pretty intense and fulfilling. I used to watch people prophesy and get lifted in the spirit as we called it. The strange thing is I was never afraid but I was very much receptive to this process. Mother had raised me in an environment of faith and Trust in God.

I remember so clearly one day in the first week of November 1969 when Mommy was in the hospital, strange things happened. People were prophesying a day or so at my aunt's house before my mother died in the hospital. Mother's health had become worse. People had come to the home because she was in the hospital.

My stepfather was there also that day. He was preparing to leave, but he was told he had to stay there to listen, and he literally could not physically move. That was a crazy and strange night at 1257 Blossom Lanes, what we called *the projects*. The night before Mother's death (November 6, 1969), I dreamed that she had died. We were going to the hospital to see her but as we were leaving we got that awful phone call. Well, that day Death showed up and my mother actually died. Mother's sickness was unto death. I cried all day that day because I wanted to see her and could not. Mother . . .

Point #22 What mommy needed to know: *I felt you leaving me even while you were in the hospital. I was preparing to come see you, and you died before I got there. I love you, Mommy. I wanted to see your warm face one more time as you smiled at me. I remember your smile and hearing you call my name, "Shirley Ann". These are beautiful memories for me.*

Point #22 What future mommies *must* know: *Your children are connected to you. If you are ill, spend some time explaining to them what is going on. Children understand more than you might realize. Your explanation and time together is so valuable. Don't take the attitude that you are sparing them pain because it is painful for you to leave unexpectedly. Remember your connection with the child began at the womb. Your heartbeat was once their heart beat as you carried them into this life. Allow them the opportunity to feel your heartbeat one more time before you leave this earth, if possible.*

What Mommy Needed To Know . . .

What Mommy Needed To Know . . .

What Mommy Needed To Know . . .

She Left Me Physically but Her Spirit Is Always Near

Mommy, I know you loved me. I am sure you know what I mean because I can hear your sweet voice reassuring me when I am by myself. I hear you saying, "Shirley Ann, I love you." Thanks Mom for loving me. I will never ever forget your love. Your love gives me the strength and courage to go on.

Your genuine love for me as your daughter is implanted in my spirit unconditionally. Even though you died at a young age and I was just a little girl I will never forget you. There are many things that I don't recall about growing up with you. One thing I truly recall is you showed so much love for me. You kept me dressed nice. You were truly a great provider.

Mother . . . I promise to keep you in my heart and make you proud of me. I really do love you Mommy. Sometimes I feel like I lacked the skills of being a better mother because I didn't have you long enough to teach me how. Don't worry though because I know I did the best I knew how. One key thing is I didn't quit or give up no matter how the wind blew and the storms showed up in my life. You gave me a solid foundation.

Point #23 What Mommy needed to know: *I love you, no matter what happened! I ache because I do not have you to talk to. I want to share my deepest secrets with you. I want to laugh with you. I want to ensure you are alright and never have a care as an elderly woman. I want to catch up on our conversations and let my children hear you tell them about my childhood. I want to hear you calling my name. Death stole you from me . . .*

Point #23 What future mommies *must* know: *Your children recall all the love you did or did not give to them. Don't let anyone poison your children's love against you. That is not a good feeling, so build and surround your children with your love always. If you don't know how to be a great mother then seek out help from creditable people.*

What Mommy Needed To Know . . .

What Mommy Needed To Know . . .

What Mommy Needed To Know . . .

Genuine Love Is Truly the Key

A mother's love is key to the success of her children. I really do still love my mother very much. I am so proud to be her middle daughter. It's like a blessing to have had her as my mother, and as a result I know that I am blessed. I am a strong woman because you were a phenomenal example. This journey in life that I began with you has not been in vain.

Mom, the next thing is I miss you very much. I have not had a mother since your departure. Of course this is obvious, but so many children think they can replace their mothers or mothers think they can replace their children. For those of you who thought you could blink your eyes three times, turn around and have a different result . . . you are wrong. This gift is for life if you have been privileged to serve in this capacity.

See I was seeking and thinking other beautiful women would fill this void this absence of mother's love. Nope, no one can fill those shoes. Fortunately I was blessed with other women who came into my life. They were mother figures. They were women who cared about me but they could never replace my mother's love. The beauty of the relationship I formed with them clearly displayed they were not seeking to replace my mom. These women were in my life for seasons to help me make it through motherhood without you. I have been blessed with beautiful, elderly women in my life. God knew what He was doing when He gave us mother. He was expressing his genuine love to us through her.

So what really is genuine of love? Can we agree that love is a learned behavior? It is one that is actually first taught to human beings by their parents. Love is first felt by the infant while in the mother's womb. So, mothers depending on how you treat yourself or allow others to treat you during your pregnancy affect your children.

It has always been said that a mother should be conscious of what she eats, drinks, how she take care of body, mind and soul because the relationship developed with her children is forming. Interestingly, what affects us affects the children. Most studies have followed the affects of alcohol, drugs, and smoking. I am certain other things whether negative or positive affect the infant children. Women now read to their children while in the womb because it is believe the children can hear and learn from their mother's voice.

We are what we eat. What thoughts are being translated to your children? Are they thoughts of how can I be a great parent for my children? Who will I reach out to when I am feeling stressed because I love my children too much to harm them. 1 Corinthians 13 is a great reading about love. Too many children are being harmed and not taught the meaning of genuine love. To say the least they are not even experiencing what they give. Children are innocent. Their hearts are made of nothing but love until someone teaches them different. Love is not a bruised butt, a black eye, broken bones or ultimately death.

Children truly live what they learn. Mothers and fathers I caution you to experience and share genuine love with your offspring. As I mentioned earlier love is a learned behavior and we can all be taught the right over the wrong. We all have the capability of loving unconditionally and with genuineness the question is "will we do it unselfishly"?

So what is genuine love to and for you?

Point #24 What mommy needed to know: *I know your love for your children was unconditional. You have never been and cannot be replaced in our lives. Thank you for loving and caring for me even while you were sick. I can recall you seeking support of someone to take care of us during your sickness because your husband would not. Wow, you were truly an extraordinary woman.*

Point #24 What future mommies *must* know: *That your children love you very much despite anything that has happened. Don't ever give up on yourself or your children. Work at forgiving them when they disappoint you, so you can really have a true loving relationship. No one can ever replace you.*

What Mommy Needed To Know . . .

What Mommy Needed To Know . . .

What Mommy Needed To Know . . .

Expressing Love Between You and Your Children

W ell, when was the last time you told your children you love them? This is very important for young children. By the way it's really cool to tell your adult children too, but you might get a different response so don't be disappointed and give up. Another mommy book will birth dealing with mothers and adult children.

This precious moment doesn't include group hugs or a casual I love you at all. Please don't take for granted that they know love them because of what you do but be assured they need to hear it. You know when you want that special person in your life to tell you that he loves you over and over and over again. What I am not speaking about is giving them gifts or things but genuinely giving them you. Material will never replace love. Materials are just that expressions of some form indicating possible love.

I know you are busy, you have to work, they get on your last nerves, you are still sorting through your own stuff, or they just don't understand you as the list goes on and on. All those things might have some truth but what really matter is . . . love. I am sure you can recall the greatest gift of all is known as this thing we call "love." There is a part of me deep within that feels and know you love your children just like I love my three children and the extensions from them.

So go ahead and ask yourself right now, "What really does matter most?" Sure, answer the question, "Do they really know I love them for them?" Don't feel guilty or proud depending on your response, just be present with your emotion and change it to make it good, better, great, or excellent. Take time to feel the love you felt when they first brought a smile to your face.

Remember when the doctor or medical person announced it's a boy or a girl, next you heard their voice for the first time. Yeah, that scream was the first time you heard their voice. Wow, what an experience!

No matter how many times you heard that new voice each time you gave birth, for the first time you knew they knew they were separated from you.

Mothers must remember this separation is only from an inside out job. Believe it or not this separation actually is an action that allows you to hold them as they hold you . . . so is it really separation or a deeper connection?

Point #25 What mommy needed to know: *I am always connected to you because I am bone of your bone and flesh of your flesh. I know I am physically separated from you but never spiritually.*

Point #25 What future mommies *must* know: *Your child cries internally or externally when they feel separated from you regardless of their age. Your children truly only wants the best for you and them. As you grow older together separation anxiety does begin to happen but this can turn out to be a positive position and not a negative position as society tends to portray. This is the beginning of a true friendship that should be known as a true BFF (Best Friends Forever).*

What Mommy Needed To Know . . .

What Mommy Needed To Know . . .

What Mommy Needed To Know . . .

Love Has a Lot to Do with It

There is this well-known saying that ask the question, "What's love got to do with it?" The saying further addresses it as a second hand emotion. Well I must say that love has a lot to do with it, wouldn't you agree. It is imperative to decipher between whether it is love and not emotions without love.

Fundamentally love is connected to emotions. This type of love is however, unique. Yes, I would challenge that unconditional love isn't tied to emotions. Emotions may appear; however, they certainly don't necessarily display the action of true unconditional love.

A mother's love makes all the difference in the lives of her children. I do hope everyone can remember when they experienced true love and dare not compare it to as a secondhand emotion. So is your love tied to your emotions? Probably and that's okay. What is not okay is to confuse the two thereby never experiencing real love.

So many things get in our way and cloud our judgment of being able to express our love purely. Did anyone ever demonstrate true love for you while you were growing up? I do not feel like everyone in my family really did after mom's death but I still made it. Sometimes mothers may have the notion that no one loves her in fact the children may even feel this way based on circumstances. Regardless to notions, potions, emotions or circumstances the truth of the matter for all to know is love is always in atmosphere. Challenge yourself to reach out and grab it. Love is in a smile.

I know someone is probably saying, "What is she talking about?" Well, I am saying just accept me for who I am without ever judging me. There were times when other people judged me based on their values and beliefs. Those times were not just in my head and it affected if I felt loved or not.

Too often we judge each other unjustly. We judge because a person does not do what we think they should be doing. We judge because we want to relive our lives through them. We judge because we just believe that we have that right to judge. School bullying is supported under auspice of judging and comparing likes or dislikes. One day my youngest adult child and I were discussing an issue. I felt very strong about my opinion and found myself judging. My son politely told me that I could not be the judge, the jury, and the lawyer too in that situation. All I could do is say, "Okay you can," but I was really regrouping because he was right. Thanks Kobe.

Point #26 What mommy needed to know: *You taught me how to be a survivor. You also showed me how to love myself, but I became insecure because of wanting to be accepted by others after you were gone out of my life. Thank you, Mom, for loving me as you did. I really appreciate it. I promise I am getting my security back and loving myself as you taught me how. I promise to not judge others, especially if it doesn't build them up for the better.*

Point #26 What future mommies *must* know: *Your children draw strength and love from you. Be sure to build them up as you cherish their qualities and gifts. They are counting on you more than anyone else. Teach them to accept others where they are and not judge them to condemnation but to restoration. Show them how to love unconditionally.*

What Mommy Needed To Know . . .

What Mommy Needed To Know . . .

What Mommy Needed To Know . . .

Love Is the Greatest of All

What does it feel like to love someone or even have someone love you unconditionally? Really, unconditionally with no strings attached. It's great when you are accepted as being just you. That, within itself, can be a strange feeling if you have never experienced it in your lifetime. How long has it been? Way too long for some of us!

Stop right now! Put the book down and tell your loved ones individually that you love and appreciate them for who they are and not what you want them to be whether they are near or far. You might have to go to the next room, or pick up the phone, or send an email or just send a shout out via Facebook or through another social media. By the way, while you are preparing to meet them and tell them, stop by the mirror, look at the person you see and say, "I love *you*!" It starts with loving yourself first.

*   *   *

Sometimes we are so hard on ourselves because someone else told us who they thought we were based on their opinion of us. What I found out is their opinion does not really matter, you might say "should not" but truly it doesn't especially if it is not building you up. Go ahead and be you. Be your best as my mother used to tell me. Don't die a carbon copy but be originally you because no one else can be like you.

Mothers you are responsible for showing love to your children. You might feel as though no one has loved you so you really don't know what it is like to give love to someone else. I am sure there was a time in your life when you really loved yourself and someone crushed that love affair. Yes, an affair with yourself. It feels great to love yourself. Your love was probably crushed when someone told you that you were selfish and arrogant because you loved you.

Did you feel resentment and vowed to never love anyone else again? I did but I also accepted that I had to love because I am love. I chose to forgive and allow myself to be love. In spite of everything I opted to not agree to let someone else control my ability to love.

Honestly before you can love someone else, too include your children you must love yourself. Many women want children to feel the void of love to later learn they were not ready for this responsibility. Children cannot replace or provide the solution for the empty spot you feel within.

The love we all long for comes from our Creator. It is totally unfair to yourself and others to be expected to fill that void. It might seem unreal, hurtful or just totally unjust for you to give someone all your love and they don't love you back. Can I comfort you to rest assure that you are loved; therefore, you can love back. You are equipped with all the tools you need to love. Let go of expecting someone else to love you on your terms and just love them for who they are. Reignite or ignite your first love affair . . . you with yourself.

When it comes to loving your children love is not imbalanced and you have the capability within yourself to love unconditionally. So again, as you share those important words of "I love you" feel the warm embrace of "love". Yes, let love flow through your very beings, to your children. Mothers, your children need, desire, deserve, and want your love unconditionally.

Point #27 What mommy needed to know: *is you shared your love with me and I am grateful. You also need to know it was so unfortunate that we didn't use those words very much in our home. In addition, I also don't believe I received enough of it or long enough. Let me whisper to the heavens hoping that you can hear me, "Mom I love you."*

Point #27 What future mommies *must* know: *is your children need to hear you love them everyday. Muster up a smile and a sweet voice that whispers I love you. Love is shown in more than material things. Love equals time, it equals sacrifice, it equals being tired and going the extra mile; it equals a radiance of . . . (go ahead you fill in the blank).*

What Mommy Needed To Know . . .

What Mommy Needed To Know . . .

What Mommy Needed To Know . . .

What Mommy Needed To Know . . .

Part III

What Mommy Needed To Know . . .

The Storms of Life

Someone once said we are either coming out of a storm, in a storm or headed into a storm in our lives. Where are you right now? Do you like where you are? You know the choice is really up to you and no one else where you are right now. You can change it as you go through the process. Yes, you and I must "go through" our storm to get to the other side of the storm. Why would anyone want to stop while they are in hell when all they have to do is make up their mind no matter what and crossover to the other side? Someone coined it as being "three feet from gold." What does this have to do with a storm? The author in this edition of Napoleon Hill's *Think and Grow Rich* starts off "informing a common cause of failure being the habit of quitting when temporary defeat seems to take over." He describes an individual who was literally three feet from the discovery of their objective, which was gold before they gave up. They were on the right course of discovering what they had set out to achieve during the gold rush but an obstacle got in the way. Instead of discovering different ways of how they could beat the odds or seeking assistance . . . they quit. After reading this book, may I suggest you pick up "Think and Grow Rich" or "Three Feet From Gold" by adding them to your library along with other great inspiring reading books. My encouragement to you is for you not to ever quit but get through your storm. You can do it. I believe in you.

Sometimes it might feel as though you are in a storm during pregnancy, while giving birth, and during the process of raising your children. The beautiful part about this feeling is it will pass. Yes, you don't have to stay there. You can muster up enough strength to get back on course and achieve your dreams even while being a mother.

Mothers are charged with raising individuals who start out from a seed implanted in their bodies that later develop to become mature individuals over a period of time. What mothers must realize and accept is your children come prewired when they enter into this world just like you and I did. Yes the nerves, cells, tissues, bones, the brain, and so forth is already present. In fact, our DNA is there also wrapped in the midst of those wires. You can't rewire your children but you are responsible for teaching your children how to properly connect the wires in their brain. How might I do this you are asking?

Well let me share with you how my mother did this while raising me. To do this as my mother did with me it is essential for you to raise your children with morals and values. The oldest book in the world known as the Bible instruct parents to raise their children in the way they should go and when they are old they will not depart (Proverbs 22:5 KJV). There are many scriptures, Proverbs, and other old sayings that provide instructions and examples on how to raise children. Lets go back to raising our children on the principles of the good ole days. Those days included respect, love, trust, and honesty among other valuable traits and characteristics.

As a young girl I recall while growing up the neighborhood on Urbandale was involved in my upbringing. Mother assumed her role as mother but she used other tools to help her raise my sisters and me. Sometimes we would go to our grandmother's house. We called her Big Mama. She would share stories about why we had to be good children and help our mother. Unfortunately, I wasn't very close to my grandmother but I knew she was there to help her daughter, my mom.

Big Mama wasn't educated but she showed love. See, it doesn't require a formal education to express the greatest gift of all, the gift of love. Love is an expression coming from within outwardly given to another only wanting nothing but the best for them. Love is happiness.

Grandmothers must be involved by sharing stories and assisting with their grandchildren. Grandmothers are just the extension of mother's hands and love to the children. Grandmothers are not to raise their grandchildren unless mothers are totally displaced out of their children's life. Don't become displaced out of your children's life. You can and should use the extension of your lineage to help you raise your children. Sit at the feet of your mother and take notes on how she made it through raising you without prejudice and judgement.

If you are here with the ability to read this book then I am certain you learned something from her. You either learned what to do or what not to do. As noted earlier mothers are a gift from God. Mothers are the only entry point into this world. Mothers who are accountable for their actions do the best they know how and when they learn better they make the choice to do better. Love your mother for who she is also and not what you want or wanted her to be.

I know I started this chapter off talking about heading into a storm, being in the storm, or coming out of the storm while experiencing life. Storms could also serve as an opportunity to transition. Become the Eye in your storm. As we progress towards the end of the book I will share different storms I experienced as a young teenage mother and forward to date. You will get the opportunity to experience through reading how I got out of the boat, crossed to the other side and conquered various storms.

I am sharing my personal experiences because I want to encourage you to take action. It is necessary for you to conquer your storms of life while you achieve your dreams and goals of life. Let me encourage or coach you to get out the boat and crossover to the other side.

Put on your life vest of love. Another person life vest might be self-confidence, self-esteem, peace of mind, understanding . . . you know your style and size. The important reminder is to get on the boat, put on your vest not someone else, and cross over to the other side. We don't want any casualties so be sure to take care of you first then help someone else. Its safe and you don't have to do it alone since there are others with the same objective.

Point #28 What mommy needed to know: is *I know you had many storms rise up in your life. Before your death I watched you strategically plan how your daughters would be taken care of during your absence. I know you didn't abandon me here on this earth without training me properly so I could make it in life. You taught me how to raise my children by not quitting on them.*

Point #28 What future mommies *must* know: is *your children must have you in their lives. You have to choose to get through the storms of life so you can assist in your children connecting their wires properly. No matter what position you might find yourself in during life it is up to you how you conquer you it. You can achieve and succeed by providing your children an example on how to raise their children. Never give up even when the going gets tough. Always be determined to get through your storm because you can. I am here cheering you on. Go Moms! Go! Fight Moms! Fight! Win Moms! Win! I believe in you . . .*

What Mommy Needed To Know . . .

What Mommy Needed To Know . . .

What Mommy Needed To Know . . .

Why Do We Feel the Way We Feel?

W hen we are embarrassed about the things that have happened to us, it generally affects our self-esteem in a negative manner. Often times when this embarrassment occurs, individuals tend to lie, run away from the situation, go into denial, or experience major life changes if the wrong person discovered or caused this embarrassment. There are so many other reasons one might be embarrassed.

Guess what? It is okay and it is a natural feeling to not deal with the situation or attempt to meet others' standards. One thing I noticed about myself is when I become embarrassed or feel ashamed about one of my choices, the little voice inside my head really beats upon me. This voice is sometimes referred to as conscious or Spirit. We all have a conscious or Spirit which operate deep within our soul, our very being. It is so deep that it speaks very loudly guiding us through life. This voice can either be negative or positive. Which voice are you listening to—your positive voice or the negative one? You get to choose, no one else. So stop saying the devil made me do it.

I begin to imagine or speak things that haven't even occurred, and my body sometimes doesn't feel very well when my negative voice shows up. I recall one time when someone made a comment about my ears and nose, which did not make me feel good about myself.

My ears are smaller than most, and my nose has its own unique shape. One time I was so embarrassed because someone pointed that out. While pointing it out there was a little chuckle, and my negative voice became a chatterbox. I found myself feeling less than the other individuals who were in my midst. Why did I take on this feeling? I was just being who I was created to be. What I failed to realize is that my features are distinct intentionally, and I am a beautiful individual inside and out. Go ahead and affirm you or who you are becoming right now. Its simple as one, two, three.

All men and women are created equal. I had to accept me for being myself. I can so clearly recall in 1987, when I was living in Washington State while serving in the US Army, the ear and nose incident helped me accept myself for who I am regardless of what others thought or said about me.

One day, in my home while looking in the mirror, I pointed to both my ears and nose, I literally told each body part that I love them. What a wonderful experience that was for me. Yes, it was a major breakthrough and a big win in my life. I had begun the process of loving and accepting myself as I was created. What I now tell myself is these are two of the sexiest parts of my body. Not only do I tell myself this, I accept it as the truth.

My truth matters more. It is not arrogance as some might say, but it is accepting myself without being concerned with anyone else's judgment or criticism. There are too many people who live their lives based on the criticisms and judgments of others. If those criticisms and judgments do not help improve and develop the real you, then cast them off into the sea of forgiveness. Forgive them for they know not what they do and keep it moving. This does require a lot of work and discipline on your part but rest assured, it can be accomplished. If you are still working on it that is a good sign to recovery and acceptance.

Is it safe to say that being ashamed of choices or decisions that we make impact our lives physically and others? This is a safe and true statement to make based on my previous experiences. I am reminded of the scripture when God walked through the garden one day to talk with Adam and Eve.

The scriptures say that He found them hiding. It is believed they were hiding because they were naked and ashamed. The story continues as God asked where they were and acknowledged they were hiding. Listen, it wasn't that God didn't know where they were but he wanted them to know where they were. Do you know where you are in life today? Knowing where you are is a key factor. You must know where you are mentally, spiritually, physically, socially, financially, and emotionally. Once you know this significant information you can access how you go there and where do you go next from here?

Why did Adam and Eve hide from God? He created them as perfect beings and there was no reason to be ashamed. Shame, guilt, and failure were emotions that over took their mindset. I believe they once had a mindset of love, power, unction, and a sense of openness with God. They had broken a personal relationship within their minds. They were ashamed because their little voice told them they were naked and had a reason to be ashamed.

Who told you that you were naked and had a need to be ashamed? Was it based on a decision you made? Was it from an abuser? Did your so-called friends and family tell you? Could it have been someone you trusted and loved very much told you when you were a kid to go somewhere and sit down. They told you that your opinion was crazy, stupid, and the dumbest thing they had ever heard or seen. Guess what? They were dead wrong. You are of such value and an intricate part to your family, to yourself, and this world. You are needed.

What they didn't realize was that you were trying to get their attention to express your true beautiful self, the uniquely designed you. The one who God broke the mold after you was made. Yes, you the "designer's original." Now children act out in the wrong way to get attention not because they were designed this way.

Mother there has been times when your decisions didn't line up with your values and morals. This normally occurs when a person is attempting to please others or be accepted at all cost. Have you ever wondered why we aim to please others more than ourselves? I find it interesting because most of my life I have attempted to please others first. Unfortunately, I often experienced hurt and regretted not thinking about me in the process of making a choice or decision. I didn't base my decision selfishly or to bring harm to another.

Now, I am sure that when I made those decisions I felt sure and confident about them. After all, at the time I told myself that I really didn't care what someone else thought of me. Or did I really care deep inside? Simply put, I believe I took the best course of action at that time based on the information I knew. "Yeah, right sure you did," is what my BIG positive voice told me! The truth be told, I really did care what others thought about me because I wanted "acceptance."

We all seek acceptance of people who we think are important or who can make a difference in our lives. We were not designed to be alone or evolve in a world that did not include others. As I moved through life I discovered that self-acceptance is more valuable and it's a huge step in the right direction for my life.

Don't misunderstand what I am saying here. I am not saying that it is not important to think of others and what others think; however, it is most important and essential that we know our value. Most times we have the answers within the depths of our spirit. Exactly, you are capable of making right choices when you are in the right mindset. Now is the time to reset your mindset.

When a child is left in a room alone with crayons, a new discovery happens almost always with the doors, the walls and possibly the floors. If it is a marker there then the child actually gets free tattoos with matching designs and colors. Yes, they get a new look. Creativity is what I will call it. The walls become the imagination of the child from inside out. The artistic ability is allowed to flow without criticism or judgment from anyone as the child discovers.

When the adult or older person enters the room, the child is asked who did this or what have they done. It is not so much what is said to the child that introduces shame or that something wrong has occurred, but it is the tone of voice used. Certain tones can register fear or embarrassment in the child's mind. Also other tones can reaffirm and comfort when heard. It can sound like a symphony or a crash. What's your tone choice?

So here we are in that what was once thought to be a beautiful creation has now turned into a moment of fear. The tone has set the temperature in the room of one being gloomy and doomed because the behavior is unacceptable. It is just as important for others to understand your tone as it is for you.

Yes, it is true children's creative mind expressed on the walls is not appropriate unless you have such a designated space in your home. The children's decision to paint a new picture or use their imagination expressed on the walls is forbidden. Most times the tone is misunderstood because it attacks the individual and not the action. Man, I wish we would think before we speak. It is so essential to speak the truth in love and let the children know you are not attacking them but their actions.

Sadly, what I discovered later is I didn't have all the information. I made some decisions based on my emotions. What I now know is that making decisions based on clouded emotions or other's opinions often are the wrong choices. I believe that emotions can be feelings used to drive your instinct to make impulse decisions when not clearly examined.

Sometimes it all boils down to something so simple as, all I needed was . . . all I ever wanted was . . . all I ever expected was . . . but I didn't expect for him or her to judge me like this or that. I thought they had my back, they were my friends, and surely they weren't making fun of my choices and me. It's hard to believe that my family had rejected me and didn't accept me for just being me—another kid on the block. Mother's these thoughts could potentially lead your children to do something drastic as commit suicide. This permanent solution is definitely not the right answer for a temporary situation. Mothers no one is exempt from these awful thoughts unless they choose not to act upon them or they are already dead. We don't have to literally die for temporary things. Lets choose to live and not listen to our negative little voice no mater its mode of transportation.

The little voice inside called me stupid or asked, "Why would you do something so outrageous?" Oh my gosh! No, they didn't do me like that, is what I felt. What am I going to do now?

Well, to tell you the truth that was many years ago but even today this negative voice still creeps inside my head. I have chosen to not let it overpower me. Many times my little voice also told me that I was okay and I was doing the right thing. Little voices in my head can sometimes be confusing. Guess what? It is okay. And you, like me, can make it. It is essential to be able to discern which voice is speaking for the greater good. It's all about choice. What are you choosing? Life or death . . .

My first moment of feeling ashamed, embarrassed, humiliated, or hopeless was when Mr. Bad, who was the father of my eldest sister's friend, molested me as mentioned earlier. I thought it was better to hide my shame and not cause hurt to anyone else. Little did I know or understand I was being hurt. Hurting people hurt others.

I felt as though what had happened to me was my fault and I had to accept my decision, despite the shame I was feeling inside. One thing I do recall so clearly was that "it did hurt." Yes, it didn't make me feel good about a choice I made. Or should I say, "A choice that was made for me, one definitely without my consent." What choice? What decision? The choice and decision not to tell anyone I was being molested on a daily basis for months. I had the power to tell but I didn't know how.

Some people would say I should have told someone. Some say, I could have said "no" to what was happening to me. Could I really? Probably, but still, I believe there were others who maybe knew, but were in complete denial because they didn't want to get involved.

The pain drove deep inside. In fact, it could still affect me mentally if I allow this ill feeling to take control. Bottom line, I was too embarrassed to tell anyone, including my dying mother. Who would believe a ten-year-old little girl? My stepfather, my sisters, his daughter, his wife? Who? I didn't know whom to turn to, so I kept it all inside. Darn! What an awful feeling for a little person to experience all alone.

It was a lonely feeling! I know that I was not alone in this dark part of the world; the disconnect was I didn't know what to do. What happened to me damaged my self-image, my self-esteem and affected future relationships with others, especially men. The silence aided in my becoming a victim of sexual abuse at an early age.

Unfortunately, many girls and boys are sexually abused every day in our society. I quoted statistics earlier. It is important to understand how many children are impacted by this horrible experience. Estey and Bomberger, LLP, states, "Statistics show that roughly 33% of girls and 14% of boys are molested before the age of 18, according to the U.S. Justice Department. Nearly 2/3 of all sexual assaults reported involved minors and roughly 1/3 involved children under the age of 12. In most cases, however, child molestation goes unreported. Estimates are that only 35% of sexual abuse is reported.

Kids can be frightened or embarrassed and many times do not say anything out of fear or just not knowing how to express their feelings." Here I was an eleven-year-old girl whose mother was dying of cancer. There was no way I could add more pain to her already-failing cancerous body. The truth is I never told her what had happened to her little girl because I didn't know how. The aforementioned stats are alarming.

Are you a victim? If you are please tell someone regardless to how long ago the incident occurred. You are in need of being healed. Mothers we can only help others when we are whole. Are you in the numbers like I was and never reported the abuse? Let me pause and encourage you to tell someone. It is never too late to change any situation or dilemma when you learn what to do about it. Seek out agencies like Estey and Bomberger, LLP, who are offering service to sexually abused children today (there is no monetary involvement for using this firm as a reference). This agency specializes in the legal field on behalf of children who are being molested. Another agency I would like to highlight is Darkness to Light. This is an agency that confronts child sexual abuse with courage. I mentioned their statistical data earlier.

As noted, these stats are unacceptable and alarming, yet they exist. Why? Are you a part of the problem or part of the solution? Mothers are you allowing your children regardless of age or even yourself deal with this horrible crime that negatively affects your or their choices made in life, silently? There is hope and people can heal from this act and not remain a victim but become victorious. Boys, girls, men and women have been attacked by this deadly weapon summarized as abuse.

I dare not talk about the incest that happened during this reading because it would just be a bit much at this time. Someone in denial might say, "Of course, those things like incest and rape really don't happen in our lives. They certainly don't in our families." Often times the truth is, they do happen but most families are in denial. *It is time to come out of denial and deal with the issues at hand. The only way things can change is to acknowledge what is happening. We are not genies nor can we wish it away and things change. We are human beings with choice and we must effectively exercise our power of choice actively. Choosing changes things.* It is not fair to punish ourselves but it is rewarding when we open ourselves up to get the help we need through invoking positive choice.

How do you eat an elephant? You are right, one bite at a time. So let's eat the elephant of rape and incest along with other cancers that are eating away at our society and families. Lets eat them one bite at a time. My pain didn't stop there. This silent abuse of sexual assault was just the beginning.

After Mom died, I just didn't feel as though I fitted in anywhere. Here I was a child who felt as though I had no decision again in what was happening to me. Mothers please know that your children are important enough to have a decision in what happens to them. Don't forget you are responsible for helping them connect the wires they were born with correctly, as they should be.

Could the reason be that children act the way they do today because they don't have a voice? They are talking and no one is listening. The language may seem foreign but if mothers would dig deep inside they can really communicate with their children on the same level.

There are many children who are like me whose mother or father hasn't died physically; however, to them their parent is dead to the situations which are happening in their lives. Is this you? Are you listening to the children who are really saying they hurt through their actions or choices? Are you even examining your own actions to understand why you do the things you do? Don't be intimidated and feel as though you will lose power if you communicate with your children. Children understand clearly who is the adult of the home. What they don't understand is when parents overpower them and feel as though they have to belittle them to prove the point. What point? The point is that the parent is in charge and responsible for their welfare. Your children want to respect and love you as you them. Work on this as a healthy mutual relationship between you and them.

Were you that child who only want to be heard and not judged? I know many of you are looking for someone to understand and reaffirm your importance in society. Interestingly, whether your role is mother, father, boy or girl, everyone is seeking to be understood and important. Well, I hope this book is giving you a great jumpstart in understanding how important you are to your family. It is also my intentions by being open and honest about my life to serve you in the highest degree. This is no fairy tale but it is truth, its my life.

Perhaps, you were not sexually assaulted, but were you physically or mentally abused? Were you rejected? Were you the kid that everyone picked on? Today's society now refers to such actions as "bullying". Did you just have a negative complex about yourself? I challenge you to do a deep internal examination of the person you see in the mirror. This process can assist you in starting your healing now. Yes, it is possible to heal. Your healing can help someone else heal, or better yet not have the awful experience.

I realize someone might not look in the mirror because it is a hard thing to do. It is okay because I am cheering and encouraging you to go the distance. I hope you can hear my voice within saying, "You are worth it all. You were chosen for such a time as this to bless the earth. You owe this new beginning to yourself. You don't have to end it all with a permanent solution." Yes, this situation you are currently facing or will face is temporary. Extra, extra read all about it . . . it is just a test and this too shall pass if you stay in the game of life.

There are many people who are looking for you to help you. Reach out. Let them take your hand and walk down this road with you. Truly it is alright. It is what is best for you and your loved ones. You are loved and love is calling your name to safety. Yes come to a safe place so you can live your best life now.

So here I was in despair with a sick mother and not old enough to take care of myself. Even though mother knew she was dying she hung in there for her girls as long as she could. One of the hand's that was reaching out to help my mother was her sister. My aunt took my sisters and me to live in her home because what else was a sister supposed to do for her dying sister? The least she could do was take her children into her home. Despite my pain, my misunderstanding, and my feeling of not belonging, I owe my aunt a huge "thank you." She kept me from becoming homeless or going into a foster care system.

Have you ever been somewhere that you felt like you had nowhere else to go? You know what I mean, like feeling trapped. Yes, that's how I felt at times in my life. I had to stay at my aunt's home after my sisters left because I had nowhere else to go except in a foster home system. There is gratitude that I did not end up in that system. I am sure my feelings had something to do with the loneliness that had entered my life through the horrific events I experienced as a little girl. How do you tell someone else what you hadn't told your mother? I didn't.

Mothers or adult care providers of children must get their children to trust them. Children must be comfortable enough to talk to their mothers and fathers. This type of communication is required of all parties involved. In today's society there are a lot of children talking with their parents; however, there are far too many who are not. It is time to open the closet, pull out the skeletons, and do a deep look inside to see what role you are playing in the communication or lack of communication process. Communication is more than talking at. It is engaged, involved, and seeking a greater understanding. This understanding will enhance and produce a healthy relationship. Great communication can occur with a lot of work.

I wanted to reach out but often I found myself keeping what I called "my problems" within myself. As a result of not wanting to rock the boat, I often found myself doing some things to the extreme to be accepted by others. How is it feasible for a child to feel as though they have problems?

Today many of our children feel as though they have problems and no one to turn to. Are you available? Would you listen to that child? Most importantly, would you give the right advice?

Children take on their problems like I did when I was young without all the valuable tools to solve problems. Not only did I not have those tools at my disposal but also I believe that I didn't have anyone who understood me. There was no one who would identify with what I was feeling.

One warning I offer to mothers is if you don't have the right advice stay quiet and just refer them to one of the agencies I mentioned or another reputable agency. I recommend you release your ego and control by directing them to the right direction. Keep the negativity to yourself. Yes, you heard me right; tell your little negative voice to "shut the hell up" cause it's not needed. It is serious to provide right guidance and counsel to those requiring it. It could be detrimental to everyone's health if ill advice is given.

Let me encourage you to seek out counseling or a confident so you can deal with your issues and get answers to your problems. Mothers we can better assist our children in resolving their problems when ours are resolved.

Children are seeking answers to their problems. Everyone has problems but not everyone has the right solution for that particular problem. Jails, drugs, dropping out of school or even walking out on life are not the best solutions. In fact, they don't qualify as sound solutions. Making quality choices is taking the high road over the low road. I challenge you to take the time to research because there are better solutions out there for everyone, regardless of the situation. I know this as a true statement because I too had to seek better opportunities and work hard at getting the best result. Never settle for just a result but go for the gold. Complete what you started with excellence, not perfection. Perfection is hard to achieve but excellence can be achieved with the right ingredients, you are the major and key ingredient.

What Mommy Needed To Know . . .

What Mommy Needed To Know . . .

What Mommy Needed To Know . . .

Shirley Ann's Life After Mother's Death

I will now share with you things about me life after my mother passed away. This segment of the book starts off sharing my pregnancy. You will get the opportunity to read about some of my storms. I plan to be up close and personal holding nothing back. This approach is intended to assist you the reader.

Thank you for sharing this journey with me. It is my prayer that I have given you valuable insight on What Mommy Needed To Know and What Future Mommies Must Know. I pray that you are able to talk with your mother sharing the truth about valuable moments with her. I further pray that future mommies and every mommy truly take the importance of motherhood to heart. Fathers, I intentionally included you because women cannot be mothers without you. Our children are crying out for both parents to be actively involved in their lives. Step up to the plate and fulfill your role as a father. No one else can do your job like you can.

Continue to jot down notes and process your life. Process what you can do to make it better because your children are depending and counting on you.

Fourteen and Pregnant

My next biggest challenge in life was that I found myself pregnant at age fourteen. Wow! What a way to begin and live life as a teenager. I was rejected, talked about by some family members and some so-called friends. It really didn't feel good for others to judge me because I was fourteen and pregnant.

After all, was it or was it not fair to me? It was too late to be judged because the damage was done. Is someone judging you and are you feeling all alone? Mothers before you judge your children look at the entire picture. If what you call "damage" is already done then don't go backwards, seek out ways to move forward. Staying stuck and criticizing only makes the situation worse. Your words either make or break your children. Believe it or not what your are telling yourself or hearing from others is either breaking or making you. There is power in what is spoken out of your mouth. Ensure your words are used wisely and for the good of others. Be cautious who you let feed your mind or your children's mind. Is it the right diet providing nourishment or is it malnourishment?

One thing I did remember is not everyone rejected me. A dear friend of the family believed in me. Interestingly this young lady was the niece of Mother Queen Lady, my mother's friend. Thanks, Henrietta. I shall forever remember your words and vote of confidence to my success.

Let me speak out for the silent voices. It's not a cool thing to not be accepted by the people you love. It might be true the people you love, are not necessarily the people, you believe love you but your words matter. Children are impressionable and deserve to have the right impression made upon them. There is truth to the self-fulfilling prophecy concept. To be accepted by those you love most is significant. Always remember, there is someone who looks up to you and love you even though they may not know how to express it with clarity. So, what I am saying is you are always making an impression on someone or someone is impressing you.

Henrietta's belief in me aided me refocusing and believing in myself. What I found out again was I had become ashamed of my choices based on what others said about me and my actions. I was ashamed due to the rejection of others after I became pregnant. Despite these feelings of rejection and being ashamed, hope was very much still alive within me.

My mother had instilled that I could make it if I tried. She not only instilled that within me but she also showed me this through her actions while living and also on her dying bed. She told me that if God opened a door for me no one could close it. She also told me that if He closed it no one could open it so become the best at whatever I chose. Mom I took your advice and it has paid off massive dividends.

High school was an eventful adventure. I took my first child to school with me every day after giving birth. I was out of school about six weeks, but I kept up with my schoolwork. I attended normal classes and I also attended parenting classes, which assisted me in becoming a good mother to my son. During those times, the school system worked for the betterment of all children regardless of the situation in which they found themselves.

In my case, I was a ninth grade young pregnant teenage mother. I am not boasting about my condition but I am proud that I didn't give up on life, on my son or on me. The school system didn't reject me; they supported me and is credited along with my mother and others in me becoming successful. Where are the teachers who genuinely care about the well-being of their students. Teachers were an intricate part of the family. My third grade teacher had some challenges but I refused to let her hinder my growth. Mrs. Shelia James, my sixth grade teacher who later became my high school guidance counselor taught me how to be a lady. I remember during middle school girls were not permitted to have hair combs in their hair and we conducted ourselves in a respectful manner. Thanks Mrs. James.

I was among the least in some people's opinion to finish school because I had two children by my senior year. I had given birth to my first child Michael at age fourteen and my second child Trenia at age seventeen. Sure, I have to agree that I was very young and yes, it was difficult, but I had a burning desire to ensure I made something of my life. My mother instilled the discipline of never quitting in me before she died. Her very actions and lifestyle spoke volumes to me.

As a mother, despite my age I was taught it is my responsibility to take care of my babies. Clearly, I am not advocating for any young girl to become pregnant as I did. In fact, I encourage you to make better choices like growing up and living your life without the additional responsibility. However, if you are a young mother let me support you by demonstrating you too can raise successful and productive children. You too, can live life at the same time.

As the middle child in my family I somewhat felt like I was alone. I felt that I had to defend the world by myself. My mother was no longer living to take care of me and I did not know my father. There was this feeling deep inside of me that I had to take care of my children, be tough, and ensure that I didn't end up as people who I loved told me I would. Some mocked, "I wasn't going to be anything or anyone in life because of my choices." I took on the role of "survivorship." I am sure you can relate if you have been in my shoes and worn that dress.

One spring my aunt met me at the bus stop and whipped me all the way home because I skipped school with a friend. I can laugh now, because I was at least sixteen years old. That particular day she had kept my son home with her because it was only a half-day of school. My goodness this was the first time I had ever skipped school and it became my only time. I didn't like the beating I had received because it was sorely embarrassing. I also accepted and realized that my aunt wanted me to succeed. Of course, I must take responsibility for my choice to skip school because I should have stayed at school.

We actually skipped and went over to a guy's house that wasn't even in school. Okay, how smart was that choice? That choice was not very smart after all. Someone once said that hindsight is 20/20. I believe this is a very true saying. My aunt knew I had skipped because the school called the house. I don't know if they got a tip or what but I do know the phone call happened.

Regardless of the choice I had made the warrior in me was still determined to make it in life. I could have never finished school without the support and encouragement of others. More importantly, I could have not finished school had I not had the determination deep within.

My determination was to make my mother proud of me, even though she was long gone from this earth. Regardless of what others thought about me, I took good care of my children to the best of my ability and help pay a mortgage. I also graduated with honors from high school. I can clearly recall saying to myself, "Mom, I know you are proud of me," as I smiled and walked across the stage to receive my high school diploma. Who do you want to be proud of you? Go ahead and follow through with making them proud because ultimately you will be proud of yourself.

The struggle was great! I won't lie. The fight to make something positive out of my life and be a good mother for my children was hard. Yet as strange as it seems, the struggle gave me the strength and willpower to continue with life. Back during the day, it was not an option to just give up on life.

So, young girls, take my word for it, yes, you can make it as a teenage mother with the right motivation and love for your children through raising them with morals and values. Nonetheless, the better choice is to just wait until you are mature and can provide for them without the assistance of the state or anyone outside of their father's support.

Let me put a plug in for the fathers who want to take care of their children without dating you. Young women, don't use your children as a weapon because you are angry with their father. I challenge you to support the involvement of the children's father in their lives. You can't play both roles; besides, we aren't equipped. If the father is abusive then use a system known as Supervised Visitation with a qualified individual.

Now, fellows, it is not my intention to leave you out or discount you. In society it is much harder for the female to overcome such challenges than it is for the male in most cases, especially being a parent. Sometimes boys are looked upon as being the "man" when they father a child. This is truly a myth and there is no truth to it if you don't fulfill manly duties by being responsible. You will find yourself in the donor category and a disappointment to your children. Your son isn't charged with being the man of the house by default. No, he hasn't fathered any children and his mother is just that, "his mother". Men stand up and be counted.

What I found out was there was a deep part in me that stood the test of rejection by surrendering my true self to live. Parenting successfully and loving my children became my motivation. I lived by continuing to accept the challenges I had chosen or those that came into my life whether I invited them or not. Life does happen. I am still working at becoming a great parent and grandparent to my family. This is possible but it does take sacrifice, work, prayer, and lots of wisdom.

What do you do when challenges show up on your doorstep? Do you quit? Run? Hide? Face it partially? Or do you face up and "take charge"? The choice is absolutely yours. You cannot blame anyone else for the decisions you had control over. Again, this only applies to the ones you had power over. By the way, if you made a bad choice, you can relook your choice and choose to do something different. You cannot undo the previous choice of choosing lemons but you can certainly make lemonade with the lemons. Add some sweetener so it's not bitter because you can take the bitter with the sweet.

There was a person trapped inside of me that always knew I could make it. The little girl inside of me had been robbed of her childhood early on in life. She didn't know who her biological father was or even spend time with him, she had been molested, lost her mother very early in life, and became a teenage mother by age fourteen. It would seem that all odds were against me and I should throw in the towel. I should have thrown in the hand that life dealt me. No, those were not options of choice because the little girl inside of me had a drive.

There was a burning desire inside of me that saw potential. There was a fight for the true person inside of me to be free. Sadly, I stayed in and out of that trapped longer than I should have because of the negative voices that spoke in my ear. I also stayed trapped because I listened to and believed my own little voice, the negative one more than I did the positive voice.

"What little voice?" you might be asking yourself. There is a voice inside your head that constantly speaks without being asked for advice. You know the voice that says things like, "you are never going to be anybody," "you're just another statistic," "you are ugly" or "too fat," "your nose is too small" or "too big," "your hair is nappy," "you are not supposed to have the best," and the list goes on and on. I am so grateful that those voices didn't destroy me even though they tried. There were times they even showed up through others.

I must admit that those negative voices impacted my life. They did affect my self-esteem; they affected my ability to think rationally and with clarity in some situations. There were times those voices were bold enough to say to me that no one cares. "It's hard, so kill yourself." Oh my goodness, I am so glad I didn't listen to that negative voice that was seeking to destroy me!

What would my children have done without their mother? How could I cause them so much pain? I couldn't imagine them having the pain of not having their mother raise them. See, in my opinion it was no one else's responsibility to raise and provide for my children but mine.

Don't get me wrong; I started off with welfare aiding me to support my children. I couldn't support myself so how was I going to support another person? I was a teenage mother true enough, but I also worked part-time when I wasn't in school. Also my eldest son's father provided support but my youngest two children's father were not involved in their lives.

I also thank my family for helping me with my children. You know the family who wasn't asked if it was okay to bring another mouth to feed in the house. You must know the family who wasn't considered in giving up their space so this new person would have somewhere to live. And the family who smelled dirty diapers or listened to the crying all night when they needed to sleep. Thank you family for supporting me and enduring the choice I made without your consent.

Now, I celebrate and acknowledge there was also another voice that encouraged me; it hugged me and it loved me and told me to "go on" because I got it in me. This voice told me that I could win. I chose to listen to this voice, so I actually won. I won because I am still here to share my story. Absolutely, we all have to make decisions and choices.

We have to ask ourselves daily, "Whose weather report are we going to believe about our life?" Ultimately, I believed the report "I could make it and I am somebody." The world is waiting on me to deliver my gifts so others could also make it.

Yes, I can recall so clearly writing the letter to my social worker saying, "Thanks, I no longer need your assistance." After graduating high school and attempting to go to college to become a lawyer, my uncle assisted me in getting my first good paying job. Hmmm, if I only knew then what I know now. Wow, there was no need to complain because the job with Whirlpool Corporation really helped me take my life to another level.

Interestingly, I left my two youngest children's father after he beat me up physically and mentally for so long. No, it's not another feel-sorry-for-me story but this led me to being physically abused by a boyfriend. He was more than a boyfriend; he was my two youngest children's father. He was a man that I trusted and wanted to spend the rest of my life with growing old since we had children together. What I learned was I had to take charge so I immediately at all cost removed him from my life. I don't regret this choice but I do regret he did not take responsibility in raising his children. I won't go on a guilt trip because that was his choice and not mine.

I started the cycle of abuse again in my life. It showed up in a different form. I accepted the maltreatment until I got tired. Yes, I do agree it should have not been an issue. But the wrong emotions played a part in my wrong decisions.

There have been times in all our lives when we sometimes accept or attempt to justify anything while looking for something, that thing we call love. Someone said . . . looking for love in all the wrong places. Actually, it wasn't love, but it was mere infatuation. Later, toward the end of the book, I will divulge what was really happening, not with him but with me.

Definitely, there was no way I was asking to be abused but I did have choices and there were signs. No, I am not blaming myself; I am just admitting that I was in denial.

My dreams weren't shattered but they were put on hold. Here, I was a young mother at twenty-one years old with three children (now adding Kobe, my youngest son) and not married. I had so many issues going inside of my head. In fact, my negative self always seem to be present. Often times I did see my positive self, reaffirming my true self by showing up being present.

It is my belief that if I had not gotten a solid foundation from watching and being taught by my mother, I would have crumbled. Who is your role model? If you don't have a role model have you asked yourself why you don't?

Role models and mentors are very important in our lives. We were designed to have someone to emulate or look up to and show us how to win at this game called life. Our dreams are often delayed but not denied. Wait a minute! Do you still dream or are you too busy with life that dreaming is no longer a part of your life?

We have what we dream when we make it a reality with focus and hard work. What are you dreaming? Are you dreaming that you can conquer the world like you did when you were a child? You know, unstoppable! I so admire the King of Pop's ability to dream. He had an imagination beyond imagining. Notwithstanding the documentaries, movies, or readings, which speak of his childhood relationship with his family, he continued to dream. Who would have thought anyone on this earth could live the way he lived? In my opinion, he cared about people and the earth we live in.

I once dreamed about becoming the first black female president. Sure, this could still happen but I have since learned that I don't want that responsibility. It is my responsibility to vote and support the leaders who are in office. Besides, if I ran for president after this book I just might win because no one would have any dirt to share about me—it's all here published.

My life turned from being molested and rejected to going to college at Lake Michigan College; Western Michigan University; Fayetteville State University, earning my Bachelor's of Science Degree in Psychology with Honors; University of Incarnate Word, earning my Master's Degree in Organizational Development; Villanova University, earning a Certificate in Lean Six Sigma (Black Belt); and Liberty University; to having the ability to work at Whirlpool Corporation in St. Joseph, Michigan, plant; and to joining the military to serve our great nation for twenty-six faithful years.

Now you may be asking, "How did you go into the military with three children?" I finally wanted to improve my life and make a change, so I left Benton Harbor, Michigan. My aunt supported my decision and took custody of my children. She became the legal guardian so I could join. One of the hardest things to do in my life was to give up the custody of my children, but I knew it was for the betterment of all at that time. I left to show them various ways of living a successful life. This exposure has enhanced their lives.

What Mommy Needed To Know . . .

What Mommy Needed To Know . . .

What Mommy Needed To Know . . .

Life in the Army

I joined the US Army in 1982. After completing my basic training and airborne school, I was sent overseas. My new life and an opportunity to change were beginning. While serving, I did experience some unique challenges as I served in our military. I experienced and overcame challenges such as racism, sexual harassment, misunderstanding, and not being supported fully when I retired after twenty-six years of honorable service by my leadership. Even with those challenges, I had the best time in my life. I served others and you with pride.

After graduating basic training, I was selected to serve as a drill corporal, jump out of airplanes, make people aware of equal-opportunity issues just to mention a few of my missions. I became the eyes and ears of the commander. I led many soldiers and ended my military career as a first sergeant. My responsibilities included, but were not limited to, leading our young soldiers, mentoring our noncommissioned officers, and supporting the officers.

Truly, my military experience changed my life and my children's lives forever. The custody separation was temporary, and my children joined me overseas. Finally, we were all together at my retirement party that turned into a family reunion. I was truly one proud mother and grandmother on that evening, yes!

Well, there was an experience that I had during my military career that truly affected not only my life but also my children's lives. I got married while I was in the military. This was truly a special time in my life. In my lifetime, I experienced a husband who was in prison, he started a thriving self-owned business, he then went back on drugs after his release, separation from one of my children mentally or at least only one confessed he felt separated from me, and suicide of a spouse. This was another time in my life that I made a not-so-good choice.

Through sharing my experiences of my married life with you, I hope to enlighten how emotions not dealt with properly affected the decisions I made. My husband was a former soldier, and we met in the Army. There has always been a wild side of me that was too scared to experience the wildness directly, but I wanted to share a part of it for some crazy reason from a distance.

Stop it! Stop judging me because we all have this in our nature. The truth of the matter is whether or not we yield and answer the voice that is calling our name. I answered that voice and married my husband after he had gotten in trouble while in the military. I had a jailhouse wedding. Yep, I did it, and I had my family and friends support my decision. Well, most of them supported. All I wanted at that time was to be married to someone whom I thought truly loved me.

Well, I must say it is my belief that my husband really did grow to love me but it wasn't his initial focus. Believe it or not, I actually grew to love him as well after we married. What a crazy way to make a choice but doggone it, I did it based on my unskilled or unclear emotions.

Visiting my husband in prison wasn't the greatest thing I had imagined for my life. In fact, if someone would have told me this story, I would have snarled or cursed. Often times, I asked myself why I did settle for this type of lifestyle. You know, I am unclear and unsure. There is a part of me that thinks I know why and I will reveal this at the end of the book. I just know that I don't regret it totally because my husband was a good man to my children and me when he was functioning without drugs.

Now, the monster that he allowed to appear in our lives was another story. Well okay, I had a monster inside of me also but I made every attempt to tame mine. I am not saying he did not attempt to tame his, but I will say that his monster won. Unfortunately, he went back to drugs, which ultimately led to his death. I won't forget the night he told me that he needed help and I didn't know what to do. I had never used crack so I had no clue on what to do or to expect. Here I go again, I was in denial. I was in denial that this elephant was way too big for me to digest.

There were several valuable lessons I learned from this marriage that has made me a better individual. I realize that in order for me to heal and be set free I must let go of any shame in my life. What I had to realize was that I hadn't done anything to go to prison. Neither did I choose to smoke a substance that took total control of my very being, leaving me with no other recourse but to answer its call when it called my name. I didn't choose to end it all by committing suicide. I am not judging or saying I was better than my husband, but I have to admit, in this case, I made a better choice.

Yes, life sometimes presents us with multiple choices but we are in charge or in control of our choices and decisions. His actions impacted everyone involved in our lives. My husband again had a phenomenal character to be a good husband and father. He was the answer to helping me deal with the molestation. I could talk to him and he understood. Little did I know but he told me that he too had been molested as a child. Nonetheless, his little negative voice brought not only danger to him but danger to everyone he loved and who loved him.

So I don't blame my deceased husband for the choices I made in my life. I accept ownership and I am very grateful to him for allowing me the opportunity to learn. Being married to him opened my eyes. After my husband's death, my eyes were truly opened to a lot of other things such as why the little girl in me disguised in a woman's body made uncalculated choices.

One major thing I learned was because I wanted to be married and have a family despite the odds with the situation at hand, that being my husband already in prison. Prison life impacts a family in more ways than one and it can actually separate a family. I was deceived in thinking I could build a successful family in this type of environment. I actually lost a valuable relationship with one of my children. How did I do that? I know that's what you're asking because I had to ask myself that when he told me.

What I failed to do was ask my children what they thought about my decision of getting married. Not only was their-mother-getting-married a welcomed or unwelcomed challenge, but I didn't ask them about having a stepfather in prison with limitation to be in their lives. My son said I forced prison into his life and he didn't have a choice.

Oh man, I repeated the molestation that happened to me when I was a young girl on my children in a different form. There is an old saying that we will repeat our actions if we don't get help and open our closed minds to see a different or the true perspective. As parents or as an adult we might believe that it doesn't matter and we shouldn't include our children in our decisions. Well, what I learned is I wasn't asking for permission to make a decision. Involving them in a process that affects their lives as little children still at home is detrimental to their well-being. Children should have a voice in matters that affect them.

My son and I are rebuilding our relationship through strengthening our communication. The valuable lesson in this situation is children really do matter and their voice is a voice we should hear. Old school days say children are to be seen and not be heard. We are truly hearing our children based on the actions we are seeing them take.

Some are doing well and making super choices. Unfortunately, way too many of our children are making themselves heard by the wrong forces and ignorant choices. Parents and adult role models, I beg you to "stop, look, listen" and take the right action. It is not the TV, Xbox 360, the government, our educational department, and our worship centers' along with other substitutes sole responsibility to raise your children.

We are the first person in the accountability line. If we don't know how to parent, it's a good thing to sign up for parenting classes. Let's take the time to truly love our children and hear what they are really saying to us not only through their actions. It is imperative to listen to their voices, feel their pain, and read their hearts.

Everything we do in life affects someone other than ourselves. We can both learn and grow from our experiences or we can stay ashamed because of what someone else will think or say to us. I chose to set myself free by not going back to work after retiring from the army and began my internal search. It was a scary process but not scarier than some of the choices I had been making in my life.

You know, I started with the woman in the mirror by being transparent with her first. I set myself free because I chose to listen to the silver lining that was within every cloud that showed up in my life. Yes, I listened to the Lord Jesus Christ as I know him.

Some may say he is the great spirit, the universe, the secret, or by some other name or action. I won't discount your belief but I just know that Yahweh has always been there to see me through. Every time I felt as though I was going to listen to my negative little voice, instantly my positive *big* voice showed up to play at one hundred percent.

After I retired, I remembered paying for some courses with a phenomenal organization. I was free to travel and attend the training that challenged me to meet another individual. I also started my network marketing business with Tahitian Noni International, became a club president at CEO Space, and my life has not been the same.

I, the individual who was once ashamed finally met this BOLD individual that was trapped inside of me all the time. I attended a warrior training, and the warrior that was inside of me came out to play. Her Warrior name is Thundering Lion Cloud. This person has never fully returned inside of me. I say fully because she fights to stay free when the negative little voice shows up with an attempt to discount her.

Remember when I said earlier in the book that I would divulge what was really going on inside of me or why I made decisions from my emotions or the negative little voice. Yes, that place where we all sometimes visit and entertain that unwanted guest. Well, during my warrior training I discovered and accepted that I felt "abandoned" as a child after my mother died.

I forgave my mother as she asked and reminded me that she hadn't abandoned me. What I know is that my mother was very ill. She had no control as to leaving me here on this earth without her. It is my firm belief that

Mommy did know that she had trained me in the way that I should go, the right way. She knew that when I grew up I would discover "me." What I also know is that all my previous actions were based on the feelings of abandonment and shame. These emotions showed up in my life as other things often in more ways than one.

I recall being listed in "Who's Who among American High School Students." That was a really great feeling, **but I didn't know who I was**. I have now adopted the attitude of it is now time to truly discover who I am, where I am going, and what my purpose is for being here on earth. I now realize why I enjoyed meeting Thundering Lion Cloud that summer day in Ellenville, New York. After meeting her and sharing those profound experiences, my life has changed for the better.

Oh my, she really was inside me all the time. I am now better able to make choices about my life. The giant has been released from inside of me, and now I am free to truly be me! I am no longer ashamed of the life that God has allowed me to live and the life I will live after. It's really a time to not only serve others but to serve me. Mothers, too often we have forgotten how to serve ourselves because of the "hustle and bustle" that life brings. When we properly serve ourselves with our children in mind then we are serving ourselves in our highest good. Yes motherhood is a sacrifice.

Mothers who inside of you do you need to loose, let go, or release so you can start your best life now? Not only that, but who do you need to acknowledge within your children that you can build and shape to love themselves no matter what?

Right now I am staying in the present, the now of my life

It really feels good to be free for I am living my best life now and I love living this kind of life. I am living my current life without fear of my past. Hello, Shirley Ann, it's great to finally meet you!

What Mommy Needed To Know . . .

What Mommy Needed To Know . . .

What Mommy Needed To Know . . .

What Mommy Needed To Know . . .

Acknowledgements

Love Expressed at All Costs No Matter What Happens or Has Happened

Great thanks go to every single person who has impacted my life whether positive or negative. It is because of you that I am what I Am. I am so grateful for this opportunity to share my life story. Yes, I took an avocado (a bland vegetable) and created guacamole one of my favorite dishes. I didn't despise my humble beginnings.

A special thank-you to my sisters, my beautiful children, and grandchildren for enduring and loving me when it was tough. Even though my husband is no longer physically in my life I am grateful for the time we shared and his ability to help me overcome certain challenges that showed up in my life. I am grateful to Mr. Berny Dorhmann for giving me the title of my book and the CEO Space family who encouraged me to step to the next dimension. I thank my entire publishing team from Xlibris. I could have not done this without you and your patience. Thanks Alison for the negotiation and website. My gratitude and thanks go to my grand daughters, Teasha, Tajah, NaTashae M-P, my dearest friend Katie H, Marysol W, Tashiana H, Keisha K, Edna B, Sharon W, LeAndrea, Yasmeen, definitely my personal assistant Je'Taime, and the many others who listened, provided feedback and encouraged me as I wrote this manuscript. To Lisa, my graphic artists, I truly appreciate you and your artistic ability as you designed my cover. Your creativity reached into me and birthed my only photo of my mom overseeing me. Your talents are commendable.

I would be disrespectful if I didn't thank Mom for giving me life. Mom, I shall forever love you. I look forward to our meeting again in the spiritual realm in a city we call heaven. Most importantly, I am grateful to my Lord and Savior Jesus Christ. Thank you for not giving up on me and remaining faithful during my times of despair. It was truly you whose footprints showed up when the sands of life seemed to dissipate beneath me.

You were all apart of the kaleidoscope of my life. The prism is my Creator, and you were all the vast colors within. My view on life has been and is great because of being afforded the opportunity to have my mother and experiencing motherhood (now grandmother of ten), which is a wonderful journey.

~Love,
Shirley Ann
a.k.a. Thundering Lion Cloud

What Mommy Needed To Know . . .

What Mommy Needed To Know . . .

What Mommy Needed To Know . . .

What Mommy Needed To Know . . .

What Mommy Needed To Know . . .

What Mommy Needed To Know . . .

Bibliography

BibleGateway. (2010). Retrieved June 10, 2010 from *http://www.biblegateway.com/*

Darkness2Light. (2010). *Child Sexual Abuse Statistics Prevalence.* Retrieved August 2, 2010 from *http://www.d2l.org/site/c.4dICIJOkGcISE/b.6143427/ k.38C5/Child_Sexual_Abuse_Statistics.htm*

Estey & Bomberger, LLP (2010). Retrieved May, 2010 from *http://www. esteybomberger.com/losangeles/sexual-abuse.php*

Feldman, R. S., (2007). *Development Across The Life Span* (5th ed.). Upper Saddle River, NJ: Prentice Hall.

Information Center for Sickle Cell and Thalassemic Disorders. (2002).*How Do People Get Sickle Cell Disease?* Cambridge, MA: Author. Retrieved September 30, 2010 from *http://sickle.bwh.harvard.edu/scd_inheritance.html*

National Center for Victims of Crime. (2010). *Child Sexual Abuse.* Washington, DC: Retrieved October 30, 2010 from *http://www.ncvc.org/ncvc/main.asp x?dbName=DocumentViewer&DocumentID=32315*

Self Help Daily Blog. (2009). *Napoleon Hill's Three Feet From Gold.* Hill, N. Retrieved October 1, 2010 from *http://www.selfhelpdaily.com/napoleon-hills- three-feet-from-gold/* (2009)

The Early Show. (2002). *Personality Traits Linked To Birth Order Place on Family Tree to Shape Personalities.* New York, NY: Neal, Rome. Retrieved September 30, 2010 from *http://www.cbsnews.com/stories/2002/06/10/ earlyshow/living/parenting/main511694.shtml*

The Oprah Winfrey Show. (2010). *200 Adult Men Who Were Molested Come Forward Part One.* New York, NY: Neal, Rome. Retrieved November 6, 2010 from *http://www.oprah.com/showinfo/An-Oprah-Show-Event-200-Men.*

Index

P

Perry, Tyler, 121
pets, 81-82, 106

R

role models, 183

S

self-acceptance, 167
sexual abuse, 169-70
  and child molesters, 120
  crimes related to, 120
  drug and alcohol problems of victims
    of, 119
  health and behavioral problems of
    victims of, 118-19
  statistics on, 117-18
  teenage pregnancy and promiscuity,
    119-20
shame, 165-69. *See also* self-acceptance
Shirley Ann
  birth, 23
  on heritage, 40, 45
  military career, 184, 188
  molestation, 169
  as parishioner, 96, 100
  pregnancy, 178
  on self-acceptance, 165-66
  skipping school, 180
  third-grade incident, 110-12
  wedding, 189

T

teachers, 9, 110-12, 179
Thundering Lion Cloud, 191-92, 198

U

Urbandale, 91, 160

V

Voice
  negative, 182
  positive, 165, 167, 182, 191

W

warrior training, 191
Whirlpool Corporation, 183-84
Winfrey, Oprah, 120

Edwards Brothers,Inc!
Thorofare, NJ 08086
09 December, 2010
BA2010343